T0193960

Night of the Confessor

Night

OF THE

Confessor

Christian Faith in an Age of Uncertainty

Tomáš Halík

TRANSLATED FROM CZECH INTO
ENGLISH BY GERALD TURNER

Image Books / New York

Published in the United States by Doubleday Religion,
an imprint of the Crown Publishing Group,
a division of Random House, Inc., New York.
www.crownpublishing.com

IMAGE, the Image colophon, and DOUBLEDAY are
registered trademarks of Random House, Inc.

Library of Congress Cataloging-in-Publication Data
Halík, Tomáš
[Noc zpovědníka. English]
Night of the Confessor : Christian faith in an age of uncertainty / Tomáš Halík ;
translated from Czech into English by Gerald Turner.—1st ed.
p.   cm.
1. Christianity and culture—Czech Republic—History—20th century.
2. Czech Republic—Church History. 3. Catholic Church—Czech Republic—
History—20th Century. 4. Religion and culture—Czech Republic—
History—20th Century. I. Title.
BR115.C8H34213 2012
274.371'083—dc23
2011022598

ISBN 978-0-385-52452-0
eISBN 978-0-307-95282-0

Book design by Jennifer Daddio/Bookmark Design & Media Inc.
Cover painting: Claude Monet, *Setting Sun on the Seine at Lavacourt,
Effect of Winter,* Musée du Petit Palais, Paris, France
(photograph © Erich Lessing/Art Resource)

First Edition

The God
Is near, and hard to grasp.
But where there is danger,
A rescuing element grows as well

— FRIEDRICH HÖLDERLEIN

Besides being wise, the Teacher also taught the people
knowledge, weighing and studying and arranging
many proverbs.

— ECCLESIASTES 12:9

Dedicated to the memory of three wise and faithful
servants of God

> *Msgr. Jiří Reinsberg (d. January 6, 2004)*
> *Pope John Paul II (d. April 2, 2005)*
> *Brother Roger of Taizé (d. August 16, 2005)*

But he said to me, "My grace is sufficient for you,
for power is made perfect in weakness" (. . .) for when
I am weak, then I am strong.

— 2 CORINTHIANS 12:9–10

Contents

Night of the Confessor

. 1 .

The Confessor's Night

The faith spoken of throughout this book (and which gave rise to it) is paradoxical in nature. One must therefore use paradoxes in order to write about it honestly and not superficially, and one can only live it—honestly and not superficially—as a paradox.

It's conceivable that some poetical "religion of nature" of the romantics or some pedagogical "religion of morality" of the Enlightenment might manage without paradoxes, but not a Christianity worthy of the name. At the core of Christianity is the enigmatic Easter story—that great paradox of victory through defeat.

I want to meditate on these mysteries of faith—as well as on many problems of our world, which these mysteries illuminate—with the help of two clues—two paradoxical statements from the New Testament. The first is Jesus' "For human beings this is impossible, but for God all things are possible";[1] the second is Saint Paul's "for when I am weak, then I am strong."[2]

The books that I have written here in the summertime solitude of a forest hermitage in the Rhineland are each of a different genre but they all have something in common: it has always been my intention to share experience from different areas of my activity and thereby also, from another viewpoint, to help diagnose the present-day climate—"to read the signs of the times."

On this occasion, as the title of the book implies, I wish to share *my experience as a confessor*. In order to forestall any misapprehensions or possible disappointment on the part of readers: this book will contain advice to neither confessors nor those who confess, and in no way will it lift the veil on what is said in confession, which is safeguarded, as is well known, by a pledge of absolute discretion. What I would like to share is how the present period—this world and its extrinsic and intrinsic aspects—is viewed by someone who is accustomed to listening to others as they acknowledge their faults and shortcomings, as they confide their conflicts, weaknesses, and doubts, but also their longing for forgiveness, reconciliation, and inner healing—for a fresh start.

For many years of my service as a priest, more than a quarter of a century, I have been regularly available for several hours, at least once a week, to people who come to the sacrament of reconciliation, or, because many of them are anabaptized or nonpracticing Catholics, for a "spiritual chat." I have thus lent an ear to several thousand people. It is likely that some of them confided to me things they had never spoken about even with their nearest and dearest. I realize that this experience has shaped my perception of the world maybe more than my years of study, my professional activity, or my travels around the seven continents of our planet. It has been my lot to have worked in a number of occupations. Every profession involves seeing the world from a different viewpoint. Surgeons, painters, judges, journalists, businesspeople, or contemplative monks, all view the world with a different focus and from a particular perspective. Confessors, too, have their own way of viewing the world and perceiving reality.

I believe that nowadays, after hours of confession, every priest who is no longer naïve and yet not cynical must be tired by the often difficult task of helping people seek the narrow, conscientious path between the Scylla of the harsh and uncompromising "thou must and thou shalt not" that cuts heartlessly like cold steel into the flesh of painful, complex, and unique life stories, and the Charybdis of the wishy-washy, speciously softhearted "everything's OK so long as you love God." Saint Augustine's dictum "Love and do what you will" is truly the royal road to Christian freedom, but it is feasible only for those who know the difficulties, risks, and responsibility involved in *truly* loving.

The art of accompanying people on a spiritual journey is "maieutical," that is, of the nature of the art of the midwife, as "care of the soul" was described by Socrates in honor of his mother (Kierkegaard adopted the term also). It is necessary, without any manipulation, to help specific individuals, in their unique situations, to find their way and arrive at a solution for which they are capable of accepting responsibility. "The law is clear," but life is complex and multivalent; sometimes the right answer is to have the courage and patience to keep asking the question.

It is usually late at night by the time I get home after hearing the last of those waiting for me in the church. I have never entirely managed to do what people in the "caring professions" are advised to do, that is, not to bring their clients' problems home with them. On occasions it can take me a long time to get to sleep.

At such moments, as one might expect from a priest, I also pray for those who have put their trust in me. Sometimes, though, in order to "retune" myself, I reach for the newspaper or the book on my bedside table, or I listen to the late-night news broadcast. And it is at those very moments that I realize that I perceive what I am reading or listening to—all those testimonies to what is happening in our world—in much the same manner as when listening to those people over the previous hours in church. I perceive them *from a confessor's perspective*, in a manner that I learned over many years both in my previous profession of clinical psychologist and even more so in my service as a priest hearing confessions. Namely, I endeavor to listen patiently and attentively, to discriminate and do my best to understand, so as to obviate the risk of asking seemingly prying questions that might be wounding. I try also to "read between the lines" and understand what people are unable (and slightly unwilling) to say in so many words, for reasons of shame, shyness, or embarrassment, or because the matter is so delicate and complicated, one that they are unaccustomed to speaking about, and they are therefore "lost for words." By then I am also searching for the right words to comfort or encourage them, or, if necessary, to show it is possible to look at the matter from a different angle and appraise things differently from how they perceive them and evaluate them at that particular moment. My questions are aimed at bringing them to reflect on whether they are concealing something fundamental from themselves. Confessors are neither interrogators nor judges; nor are they psychotherapists—and they have only a limited amount in common with psychologists. People come to confessors in the expectation and hope that they will provide them with more than is implicit in their human skills, their specialist education, or their practical experience, both "clinical" and personal—that they have at their disposal words whose sense and healing power emanate from those depths we call the sacrament: *mysterion*—the sacral mystery.

A confessional conversation without a "sacral dimension" would be mere psychotherapy (and often amateurish and superficial to boot). On the other hand, a mechanically performed "sacrament" and nothing more, without any context of human encounter, in the sense of conversation and keeping company in the spirit of the Gospel (as Christ did when he accompanied his sad and confused disciples on the road to Emmaus), could degenerate into something akin to mere magic.

People sometimes come to a confessor, at least to the confessor whose confession this book is, in situations in which their entire "religious system"—their thinking, their experience, and their behavior—is in a greater or lesser state of crisis. They feel themselves to be in a "blind alley" and are often unaware whether it happened as the result of some more or less conscious or self-confessed moral failing or "sin," or whether it is to do with some other changes in their personal life and relationships, or whether they have only now realized the outcome of some long and unperceived process during which their faith dwindled and guttered out. Sometimes they feel a void, because in spite of their sincere endeavors and often long years of spiritual search they have not found a sufficiently convincing answer in the places they have looked so far, or what had so far been their spiritual home has started to seem constricted or spurious.

Despite the uniqueness of individual human stories, after years of practice as a confessor one discovers certain recurrent themes. And that is the second aspect of the confessor's experience to which this book seeks to provide a testimony. Through the multitude of individual confessions, which are protected, as has been said, by the seal of absolute discretion, the confessor comes into contact with something that is more general and common to all, something that lies beneath the surface of individual lives and belongs to a kind of "hidden face of the times," to their "inner tuning."

It is particularly when you accompany young people on their spiritual journey that you have access to a kind of seismograph enabling you to gauge to a certain extent impending

tremors and changes in the world, or a Geiger counter recogniz-
ing the level of spiritual and moral contamination within the
society in which we live. It sometimes strikes me—even though
I'm very rationally minded and have a powerful aversion to the
fashionable shady world of occult premonitions and spiritualist
table tapping—that the events that subsequently erupt onto the
surface and shake the world, such as wars, terrorist attacks, or
even natural disasters, have some kind of analogy or even au-
gury in people's *inner world* and are presaged long in advance by
changes in the spiritual lives of many individuals and the "mood
of the times."

In that sense, therefore, my very extensive, although also
limited, "confessional experience" colors my view of contemporary society. I constantly compare it with what is written by
my professional colleagues: philosophers, sociologists, psychologists, and theologians, as well as by historians and journalists,
of course.

At a time when evil is becoming globalized in a striking
fashion—its most blatant manifestation being international terrorism, although natural disasters also constitute one aspect of
it—and our human intellect is incapable of sufficiently grasp-
ing these phenomena, let alone averting them, there seems little
chance of resuscitating the optimism of the modern era. Our
epoch is definitely a *post-optimistic* one.

Optimism, as I understand it, is the conviction that "everything is OK," and a naïve tendency to trust that *something* will
ensure that things will get better and better—that if, at this moment, we don't happen to be living in "the best of all possible
worlds," we shall soon achieve that *optimum*. That redemptive
"something" that optimism relies on can be scientific and technological progress, the power of the human intellect, revolution,
social engineering, various schemes dreamt up by "engineers of
human souls," or pedagogical and social experiments in social

reform—this is the secular version of optimism. But there also exists a religious version of optimism, which consists of reliance on a consecrated stage director who extricates us from our problems like a "deus ex machina," because, after all, we have reliable tools (all we need is to "believe with all our strength" and hold "prayer crusades") whereby we can induce Him to satisfy our requests infallibly.

I reject secular and "pious" optimism alike, on account of both their naïveté and their superficiality, and because of their unavowed striving to make the future (and possibly God) fit into our limited visions, plans, and perceptions about what is good and right. Whereas Christian hope is openness and a readiness to search for meaning in what is to come, I sense at the back of this caricature a cockeyed assumption that we always know in advance, after all, what is best for us.

Much has already been written about the naïveté of secular optimism (an Enlightenment faith in "progress" as the panacea) and its failure. However, I would like to take a stand against "religious optimism"—*facile belief,* making use of people's anxiety and suggestibility for a manipulatory "bargain with God," and providing simplistic "pious" answers to complex questions.

It is my deeply held belief that we must not conceal our crises. We must not evade or elude them. And we must not let them scare us. Only when we have passed through them can we be "remolded" into a state of greater maturity and wisdom. I would like, in this book, to show that the crisis of the world around us, and also the "crises of religion" (whether that is taken to mean the decline in the influence and stability of traditional religious institutions, the dwindling persuasiveness of existing systems of religious interpretations of the world and faith, or personal crises in "spiritual life") are enormous windows of opportunity opened to us by God. These are challenges for us "to put out into the deep."

I regard the awakening of just such an attitude to life—not avoiding crises but *taking up one's cross*—to be one of Christianity's most valuable contributions. Christianity is not primarily "a system of dogmatic texts," but instead a *method*, a way, a route.[3] Following the way of the one who did not evade the darkness of Gethsemane, Good Friday, or the "descent into hell" of Holy Saturday.

Every Christian has heard plenty of reflections and sermons on the theme of the Easter events, but has Easter really become the key to understanding our life and the present situation of the Church? For many of us "the cross" tends to evoke purely personal problems, such as illness and old age. I fear that the notion that *a great deal within ourselves, within the Church, within our faith, and within our certainties has to "die off," to be crucified, in order to make room for the Resurrected one* is quite alien to many of us Christians.

When we confess the Easter faith, at whose center is the paradox of victory through an absurd defeat, why are we so afraid of our own defeats—including the demonstrable weaknesses of Christianity in the world of today? Isn't God speaking to us through these realities, similar to the way He did when He spoke through the events that we commemorate when we read the story of Easter?

Yes, the form of religion that we are accustomed to is truly "dying off." The history of religion and the history of Christianity consist of periods of crisis and periods of renewal; the only religion that is truly dead is one that does not undergo change, the one that has dropped out of that rhythm of life.

It is not by chance that the Christian thinkers whom we might term "theologians of paradox"—such as Saint Paul, Augustine, Pascal, or Kierkegaard—all lived at crucial moments in the history of faith, and through their interpretations they were able to indicate "the signs of the times" and open up new scope for the life of faith: Paul at the moment when early Christianity parted ways with Judaism, Augustine amid the turbulence after the fall of Rome, Pascal in the upheavals that gave rise to the modern world, and Kierkegaard when this world of mass civic Christianity of modern times was finally beginning to fall apart.

At the present time, as I shall try to show in several places in this book, we are witnessing the withering away of a type of religion (and Christianity) that came into existence at the time of the Enlightenment—partly under its influence and partly in reaction to it. It is withering away with its epoch: "modern times." As on many occasions in history, this situation of faith can be interpreted "optimistically" or "catastrophically": the "optimistic" interpretation offers various "technical solutions" (a return to premodern religion or a facile "modernization of religion"). The catastrophic vision speaks (yet again) of Christianity's final demise.[4] What I'm attempting here is a totally different approach to "our present crisis": I shall endeavor to interpret it as "an Easter paradox." The mystery of Easter forms the very *nub of Christianity,* and precisely within that I see a *method* of dealing with the present "problems of Christianity," religion, and the world in which we live.

The deliberations in this book seek to take the *theology and spirituality of paradox* a step further. What I describe as "the theology of paradox" can be traced throughout the tradition of Christian thought from the apostle Paul, Tertullian, Origen, and Augustine, then on through Dionysius the Areopagite and the whole tradition of "negative theology" and the philosophical mystics, from Meister Eckhart to John of the Cross, and from Pascal and Kierkegaard to today's "postmodernists," John Caputo and Jean-Luc Marion, or my favorite author Nicholas Lash. It is evident also in Jewish mysticism and theology from the earliest times up to modern Jewish thinkers, particularly Martin Buber, Hans Jonas, and Abraham Heschel. Analogously with "deep psychology" and "deep ecology" we might perhaps speak about *deep theology*—that is, the kind that emphasizes "the hiddenness of God."[5] My reflections seek to demonstrate that the *paradox* of faith is not simply a topic for theological speculation; it can also be "lived" and become the key to understanding the spiritual situation and challenges of our times.

The "Paschal Mystery" is the source of the *power* that has been entrusted to confessors, the power to "bind and loose," and heal the wounds caused in the world by evil and guilt. Whenever I use the words of the absolution, the ones I find of greatest substance are: "through the death and resurrection of his Son."[6] Without this "power of Easter," confession (and the entire sacrament of reconciliation) would really be no more than what it is imagined to be by outsiders—an opportunity to "unburden oneself," get things off one's chest, let off steam, seek advice—in other words, something for which one could easily substitute a wise woman or a psychoanalyst's couch. In reality the sacrament of reconciliation is something else entirely, something much deeper: the healing fruits of the Easter events.

When the apostle Paul started to talk to the Greeks on the Areopagus in Athens about the meaning of Easter and the mystery of the Resurrection, most of them turned away from him in scorn because they thought they already knew plenty of myths like that. They gave him no opportunity to explain that he meant *something entirely different* by the expression "resurrection from the dead" than what they imagined and scorned. Only a few of them, a certain Dionysius the Areopagite, his wife, Damaris, and several others, stood by Paul.[7]

I ask myself: How many such Dionysiuses can I expect among my readers, now that I intend, up to the end of this chapter (which I expect to be the "hardest" passage of the entire book), to embark on reflections about the same mystery, which is shrouded in so many misapprehensions?

It is news of the Resurrection that marks the moment when the Gospels become "good news" (*euangelion*), a liberating message of salvation—the resurrection that even the disciples initially found unbelievable and impossible. It is not surprising; it definitely is "impossible," in the sense, at least, that something of the kind is beyond the possibilities of human action or human understanding. It is radically different from anything that we or any other human being has experienced. Jesus's Resurrection in the biblical and theological sense is not the "resuscitation of a corpse," a return to a former state, to this world, and to this life that once more ends in death. The New Testament authors, and particularly the profoundest of them, Paul, were at pains to ensure that we do not confuse these things.[8] The Resurrection of Christ is not another miracle such as the marvels familiar to every reader of the Bible. This concept (image or metaphor, if you wish, because all attempts to speak about God rely on images and metaphor[9]) means *much more*. That is why this message—the Gospel about the Resurrection—demands a much more radical response from us than simply forming an opinion about what happened to Jesus's corpse; first and foremost it is necessary to do something about our own lives: we, too, must undergo a profound change, in Paul's words "to die with Christ and rise from the dead." Belief in the Resurrection implies the courage to "take up one's cross" and the determination to "live a new life"; only when the event, of which the Easter story speaks, transforms our existence does it become "good news" for us, words "full of life and strength."

The Easter story can be read in two quite different ways. Either as a *drama in two acts*: in the first act a just and innocent man is sentenced to death and executed, and then, in the second act, is resurrected and accepted by God. Or as a *drama in one act* in which both versions of the story take place at the same time.

In the first interpretation the "Resurrection" is the happy ending, and the entire story is a typical myth or optimistic fairy tale. I can hear a story like that and think to myself that that was more or less the way it happened (which people confuse with "faith"), or I can conclude that it didn't happen like that—or at all (which people confuse with "lack of faith").

Nevertheless it is the second interpretation, the "parallel" one, that is actually *reading with the eyes of faith. Faith* here means two things, however: on the one hand, *the realization that the story is paradoxical* (that the other aspect of the story, "the resurrection," is a *reinterpretation* of the first, not its subsequent happy outcome[10]); and on the other, *the determination to link that story to the story of one's own life.* That means "to enter into the story" and in the light of it to understand and live one's life afresh, to be capable of bearing its paradoxical character, and not to fear the paradoxes that life presents.

The second interpretation of the Easter story does not involve "optimism" (the *opinion* that everything will somehow turn out all right), but *hope:* —the ability to "reinterpret" even things that "don't turn out all right" (after all, life as a whole can be regarded as "an incurable disease necessarily ending in death") so that we may accept reality and its burden, persist in this situation, and stand the test—and where possible be useful to others also.

The mystery of the Resurrection is not a feel-good happy ending, canceling and annulling the mystery of the cross. One of the great theologians of the twentieth century, J. B. Metz, emphasized that when we proclaim the message of Resurrection "we must not silence the cry of the Crucified"; otherwise instead of a Christian theology of Resurrection we offer a shallow "myth of victory."[11]

Belief in the Resurrection is not intended to make light of

the tragic aspects of human life; it does not enable us to avoid the burden of mystery (including the mystery of suffering and death), or not to take seriously those who wrestle strenuously with hope, who "bear the burden and the heat of the day" of the external and internal deserts of our world. It does not assert some "religious ideology" and *facile belief* in place of following in the path of the crucified Christ. Indeed, the facile belief that we are offered on every side these days is, in my view, the most dangerous infectious disease from which we should protect Christianity and our own individual spiritual journeys.

A failure to comprehend the paradoxical nature of Christianity leads either to inane "scientific atheism" (proving that all of it "isn't true") or to the no-less-inane apologetic argumentation (would-be rational and unconflictual) that it is all true (such as booklets with such titles as *The Bible as History*), without either of them asking questions about *how* things are or are not true and *what is the nature* of that truth that is revealed here and also remains hidden.

Understanding the paradoxical nature of Christianity can mean more than just getting inspiration for writing interesting texts—although this it certainly does, because literature, philosophy, and theology are only interesting if they tackle paradoxes and do not censor either one aspect or another of reality; this reading can be "inspiration for life."

In this book I will speak about faith chiefly in terms of *a specific sort of attitude to reality.* My experience, including my experience as a confessor, has taught me to differentiate between *explicit* and *implicit* faith. Explicit faith is the fruit of reflection; it is conscious and expressed in words. Yet even people who do not espouse a faith sometimes display in their behavior "implicit" present values that are fundamental to an attitude of faith.

In various places the New Testament states that the only

faith that will stand the test with God is *lived faith.* God values attitudes, behavior, and deeds that accord with the truths of faith—even when they are not explicitly the outcome of "conscious religious motivations." On the other hand, *mere* "conviction," if it is not embodied in life, is simply hypocrisy in His eyes—a "dead faith."[12]

When we are speaking about the discrepancy between "religious conviction" and "life," let us not focus solely on the downright "hypocrites" that Jesus spoke about when castigating the Pharisees. After all, we Christians are all sinners who have greater or lesser deficits and debts with regard to what we proclaim.

In short, what people do in and with their lives is not a mechanical reflection of their opinions (including religious opinions); on occasion we can sometimes be surprised, both agreeably and otherwise. One of Sigmund Freud's loyal friends and pupils, the protestant theologian Oskar Pfister, gave his teacher the following answer when asked if a believing Christian can be tolerant of atheism: "When I reflect that you are much better and deeper than your disbelief, and that I am much worse and more superficial than my faith, I conclude that the abyss between us cannot yawn so grimly."[13]

None of this means that I wish to belittle in any way the formal aspects of explicit Christianness. The relationship between "implicit" and "explicit" faith is a complex one. I would simply like to point out that we should eschew too black-and-white a vision and the simplistic drawing of boundaries.

In one of the subsequent chapters I will try to demonstrate that a certain attitude to the world that indicates that the person truly perceives it as a gift in trust can be designated an *attitude of faith.* And by the same token certain "lifestyles" indicating that people are "their own god" or that they have deified (absolutized) some partial value are both "idolatry" and the opposite of an attitude of faith. I consider *piety* to be openness to the unmanipulated mystery of life.

The God referred to in this book—and the author is firmly convinced that it is the God spoken of by Scripture and the Christian tradition (and he calls as witness many great thinkers in that tradition)—is not a "supernatural being" somewhere in the wings of the visible world,[14] but a mystery that is the depths and foundation of all reality. If we steer our life toward Him, then our life (and our attitude to life and reality) *is transformed from a monologue into a dialogue*, and what seemed impossible to us becomes possible.

In this book the "Kingdom of God" will be referred to as the "kingdom of the impossible," because it consists of much that rightly appears to human intellect, human imagination, and everyday experience as *impossible and unimaginable.* In many life situations Jesus wants us to act "impossibly" in terms of the logic "of this world," which is a world of cunning, selfishness, and violence. He wants us to forgive where we could take vengeance, to give where we could keep for ourselves, to love those who do not love us and are not "lovable," to take action in favor of the poor who cannot pay us back, when we could, calmly and unperturbed, continue to lounge around in our pleasantly cozy indifference and detachment.[15] Jesus is not content with dazzling us with "impossible feats," spectacular miracles, fascinating visions, and unprecedented theorems, as others have done and continue to do; he wants us to imitate him, to be *agents of the impossible*: "whoever believes in me will do the works that I do, and will do greater ones than these, because I am going to the Father."[16]

Only faith, love, and hope, which are the heart of the Christian existence, can offer this new opportunity where, with human eyes, we have ceased to expect it: hope in the Christian sense, says the apostle Paul in one of his many paradoxical statements: means "hoping against hope."[17] This is because they are based on a great paradox preached by Jesus of Nazareth (and which permeates the entire Bible): what is impossible with people is possible with God. *Nothing is impossible with God.*

What I have just said in a condensed and abbreviated way in the preceding paragraphs is more or less the message of this entire book. Those who have made up their minds long ago about all this and have no need or wish to reflect on it do not have to take the trouble of reading it. Those for whom this outlook is fundamentally unacceptable and regard it from the outset as nonsense or wrong, and are staunchly certain of it, should probably not waste their time either. But those who regard these few thoughts as *worthy of reflection* and are prepared to suspend for the time being the moment of agreement or disagreement, are very welcome to proceed further. They must expect to hear what was said in the previous paragraphs several times over in different variations, in various contexts and from different angles.

I hope that the following essays will provide readers with opportunities for careful *reflection* (on the world around them, on the mystery of faith, and on themselves), that it will sometimes induce moments of quiet *contemplation*, and also moments of pleasant *amusement*—because the writer experienced these three great joys when penning them.

Give Us a Little Faith

"You have come here not to acquire something, but to discard a lot of things," an old and experienced monk told a novice who sought him out in the monastery. I recalled those words yesterday when I once more set foot in the hermitage for the first time in a year. And the same thought struck me this morning when meditating on the Gospel passage in which the disciples say to Jesus, "Increase our faith!" and Jesus replies, "If you have faith the size of a mustard seed . . ."[1]

Suddenly this text spoke to me in a way that differed from the usual interpretation. Isn't Jesus saying *to us* with these words: Why are you asking me for *lots of* faith? Maybe your faith is "far too big." Only if it *decreases*, until it is as small as a mustard seed, will it give forth its fruit and display its strength.

Tiny little faith need not necessarily be simply the fruit of sinful lack of faith. "Little faith" can sometimes contain more life and truth than "great faith." Can't we apply to faith what

Jesus said in the parable about the seed that must *die* in order to bring great benefit, because it would disappear and be of no use were it to remain unchanged? Does not faith also have to undergo a time of dying and radical diminution in the life of man and in the course of history? And if we apprehend this situation in the spirit of the Gospel's paradoxical logic, in which small takes precedence over big, and loss is profit, and *diminution, reduction* means openness to the advancement of God's work, isn't this crisis actually the "time of visitation," *kairos,* the opportune moment?

Perhaps we have too hastily attributed a "divine" connotation to many of the "religious matters" to which we have become accustomed, when in fact they were human—all too human, and only if they are radically reduced will their truly *divine* component come into play.

A thought that had been germinating within me for years, as a kind of vague presentiment, suddenly burst forth with such urgency that it could no longer be suppressed.

And because I have a lasting concern not only for Christians who have a settled place within the church, but also for those spiritual seekers outside the church, it occurred to me that we maybe owe those people in particular that "little faith" if we are at last to offer them bread in place of a stone. And in view of the fact that many of the things to which we have become overaccustomed are alien to them, are they not precisely the ones who are most inclined to understand this "little faith"?

No, I really am not proposing some kind of simplified, "plain," "humanized," and facile Christianity, let alone some romantic or fundamentalist "return to the origins." Rather the opposite, in fact!

I am convinced that it is precisely a faith tempered in the fire of crisis and divested of those elements that are "too human" that will prove more resistant to the constant temptations to simplify and vulgarize religion, to sell it short.

The opposite of the "little faith" I have in mind is actually "credulity," the overcasual accumulation of "certainties" and ideological constructions, until in the end one cannot see the "forest" of faith—its depth and its mystery—for all the "trees" of such religion.

Indeed, during these days of reflection in the solitude of a forest, I am attracted to the image of the *forest* or *woods* as an apt metaphor for religious mystery—a forest that is broad and deep, with its fascinating multiplicity of life forms; a multilayered ecosystem; an unfinished symphony of nature; a spontaneously intricate space—such a contrast to planned and premeditated human settlements with their streets and parks—a place in which one can get lost over and over again, but also discover to one's surprise still more of its aspects and gifts.[2]

A "little faith" is not an "easy faith." My greatest encouragement on this path of understanding faith was Carmelite mysticism—from John of the Cross, who taught that we must go to the very limits of our human "spiritual capacities," our reason, our memory, and our will, and only there, where we feel we are in a blind alley, do true faith, love, and hope come into being; and along the "small path" of Thérèse of Lisieux, which culminated in the dark moments of her dying.

My question is whether our faith, like our Lord, is not required to "suffer much, be crucified, and die" before it can "rise from the dead."

What does faith suffer from, what crucifies it? (I am not referring to the external persecution of Christians.) In its primal form ("primary naïveté" in Paul Ricœur's words)—that is, in the form that must one day expire—faith suffers above all from the "multivalence of life." Its cross is the profound ambivalence of reality: the paradoxes that life brings, which defy systems of simple rules, proscriptions and prescriptions—and that is the rock against which it frequently shatters. But isn't it possible that, in terms of its meaning and outcome, such a moment of "fragmentation" can be like when we crack open a nut in order to get at the kernel?

For many people, this "simple faith"—and the "simple morality" derived from it—finds itself in serious crisis when it comes up against what must sooner or later confront it, namely, the complexity of certain life situations (often to do with human relationships) and the impossibility of choosing out of the many possible options one solution that involves no "buts" of any kind. The result is "religious turmoil" and paroxysms of doubt—the very things that this type of faith cannot cope with.

When confronted by the barricade of their own unanticipated doubts, some believers "turn back" in the direction of the expected safety of their beginnings—*either the "childish phase" of their own faith or some imitation of the Church's past.*

Such people often seek a haven in sectarian forms of religion. Various groups offer them an environment in which they can "pray down," shout, weep, and clap themselves out of their anxieties, and experience a psychological regression into "baby talk" ("speaking in tongues"), as well as be cradled and caressed by the presence of people of like tendency and often with even bigger problems.

Then there are various "folk museums" of the *Church's* past on offer; they try to simulate a world of "simple human piety" or a type of theology, liturgy, and spirituality of past centuries "unspoiled by modernity." But the dictum "you can't step into the same river twice" applies here, too. In most cases it proves in the end to have been just a romantic game, an attempt to enter a world that no longer exists. Attempts to find a home in illusions tend to go hand in hand with desperate efforts to pretend to oneself and to others. It is just as fatuous for an adult to try to enter the nursery of his childish faith or to retrieve the primal enthusiasm of the convert as it is to try to overstep the bounds of time and enter the spiritual world of premodern religion. The folk museum that people thereby create is *not* a living village of traditional human piety or a medieval monastery. It is a collection of romantic projections of our notions of what it was like when the world and the Church were "still in order." They are simply pitifully comical caricatures of the past.

"Fundamentalism" is a disorder of a faith that tries to entrench itself within the shadows of the past against the disturbing complexity of life. Fanaticism, with which it is often linked, is simply a peevish reaction to the resultant frustration, to the (unadmitted) bitter realization that it is a false trail. Religious intolerance is often the fruit of covert envy of others, those "outside," an envy that proceeds from the embittered hearts of people who are unwilling to acknowledge their sense of profound dissatisfaction with their own spiritual home. They lack the strength to change it or abandon it, and so they cling to it desperately and try to shift offstage everything that might recall possible alternatives. They project their own unacknowledged and unsolved doubts onto others and struggle with them there.

Often faith that appears "great" and "firm" is in reality simply leaden, solidified, and bloated. Often the only great and firm thing about it is the "armor plating" that frequently conceals the anxiety of hopelessness.

The faith that undergoes the fire of the cross without retreating probably loses much of what it tended to be identified with or what it was itself accustomed to, even though it was merely superficial. Much will be scorched away. However, its new maturity will be chiefly evident from the fact that it will no longer appear "in armor"; instead it will be a bit like that "naked faith" that the mystics speak of. It will not be aggressive or arrogant, let alone impatient in its relationship with others. Yes, compared to "great" and "firm" faith it may appear small and insignificant—it will be like *nothing*, like a mustard seed.

But that is precisely how God operates in this world, says Meister Eckhart: He is "nothing" in a world of beings, because God is not a being among beings. And Eckhart goes on to declare that you must become "nothing" if you wish to encounter Him. If you want to be "something" (that is, mean something, have something, know something, in short, be fixated on individual beings and the world of things), then you are not free to encounter Him.

Maybe our faith, too, was overwhelmed with lots of things, which had the nature of that "something"—our personal notions, projections, and wishes, our all-too-human expectations, our definitions and theories, the world of our stories and myths, our "credulity." Maybe we have not yet had our fill of all that and we want more: Give us *more* faith, more certainty and assurance in the face of life's complexities!

But Christ says: "Have the faith of God,"[3] not the "human" kind that could become lost among the ideologies and philosophies of our times. A "God kind of faith" means one that is minuscule, almost imperceptible, from the point of view of this world!

God, who is preached and represented in this world by the One who was crucified and rose from the dead, is the God of paradox: what people consider wise He considers folly, what people regard as madness and a stumbling block is wisdom in His eyes, what people see as weakness He considers strength, what people consider great He sees as small, and what they find small He regards as great.[4]

Are we, even in the blasts of the gale that continues to blow away so much of our religion—whether we have in mind the onslaught of atheistic criticism or the tempest of our own doubts and inner crises of faith, or the "spirit unfriendly" climate of the times—capable, in the end, of discerning the liberating gust of the Holy Spirit just as the Israelites, thanks to their prophets, were able to discern "God's lesson" in their defeats and "God's servant" in their enemy Nebuchadnezzar?

When human beings, or "God's people," are not capable of abandoning something that binds them and encumbers them for the future journey, the Lord sometimes resorts to methods of deliverance that we definitely do not find pleasant. "*Zugrunde gehen*," as we know from Nietzsche, means not only running aground and disappearing, but also literally "going to the foundations" and touching the core.

And so I close this first meditation with a prayer: Lord, if our religiosity is overburdened by our certainties, take some of this "great faith" away from us. Take from our religion that which is "too human" and give us "the faith of God." Give us rather, if it be Your will, a "little faith," as small as a mustard seed—small and full of *Your* power!

. 3 .

Kingdom of the
Impossible Come

What does Christ promise for "little faith"? The Gospel text that
I meditated on yesterday was deliberately not quoted in full, because I did not want the second part of it, which is very striking
and provocative, to draw attention away from the words about
"little faith" as it used to do for me whenever I read the passage.
So now let's read the entire passage: "If you have faith the size
of a mustard seed, you would say to this mulberry tree, 'Be up-
rooted and planted in the sea,' and it would obey you."[1]

So what does Jesus promise? Something impossibly absurd.

A friend of mine told me how, when he was a little boy, similar words of Jesus's induced him to go off to a meadow beyond
his native village and fix his eyes on a huge mountain. With extreme concentration, he summoned up all the strength of his
utterly sincere and fervent faith and commanded the mountain
to move in the name of Jesus. I hasten to assure the eager reader

that nothing at all happened—apart from the fact that the lad "lost his faith" for a few years.

Yes, it's a funny story, of course. We are not naïve children; we know that Scripture cannot be taken literally, that Jesus was using a Middle Eastern language full of hyperbole. This is a case where even the most obdurate fundamentalist would hardly take Jesus literally and seek to command mountains or trees to move through the power of their will, without technical assistance. But where does that leave us with this statement?

A frequent interpretation is that Jesus was promising firm believers that they would be capable of accomplishing great and admirable deeds. Nowadays Christian groups that promise "exceptional gifts of the Holy Spirit" are extremely popular. Who, especially the spurned and complex ridden, wouldn't be tempted to satisfy their covert narcissism, megalomania, Messiah complex, admiration starvation, sense of being chosen, or whatever? Who wouldn't like to appear in stadiums before fascinated crowds and drive out demons, cure people's various diseases by prayer or the laying on of hands, and provide the drug-dependent or mentally sick with a quick alternative to years of therapy—and all the while have the feeling that "it isn't by their own virtue"—that they are simply engaged in selfless and sacred service to others? Yes, this, too, is a way of interpreting these (and many other) words of Jesus—as a promise of performing spectacular "miracles"; you just have to believe the right way, that's all![2]

A similarly erroneous, and alas widespread, interpretation of these words consists in confusing "strong faith" with autosuggestion. The "Silva Method" and many other similar programs teach us fairly easily and quickly—for a hefty fee, of course—to train "the hidden powers of our mind," or help us achieve outstanding success (or, what is more common, help us convince ourselves that we really are successful and convince the more gullible around us of that fact). These programs are often spiced with biblical quotations and references. In this way faith in the biblical sense, trust in the Lord is replaced—with similar ease, speed, and success—by something that is its total opposite: a technique of maximum self-affirmation, self-assertiveness, and the "extension of one's own potential." Without wishing to offend the many truly sincere Christians in the United States, whenever I hear of America's great "devoutness" being put forward as an example for secular Europe, I always recall with a shudder the words of the contemporary American philosopher Richard Rorty that Americans have not abandoned faith; they have done something else: they have *redefined God*; when they say God they mean "our future selves."[3]

I don't doubt in the least that one can influence people's subconscious with appropriate techniques, that autosuggestion can affect human performance, and so forth and so on, but I definitely radically reject the view that autosuggestion is "actually more or less the same" as what the Bible means by *faith*.

Jesus truly does promise that "a faith as small as a mustard seed" will achieve something impossible and absurd, something unprecedented and unthinkable. But it is not a matter of either "exceptional deeds" or the "miracles" and "exceptional gifts of the Spirit" expected by those who chase after sensations. The most radical expressions of faith—truly absurd and impossible, indeed foolish and crazy *in the eyes of "this world"*[4]—don't look anything like that. They include forgiving when I could take vengeance, and even "loving my neighbor" and "turning the other cheek" when I have been done wrong to; giving away things that I could happily keep for myself; being generous above all to those who are unable to pay me back; giving up "for the sake of the Kingdom of God" something that others consider an essential part of a happy life.[5]

In the eyes of *this world*—and let's face it, in our eyes too, depending on the extent to which we are part of it and influenced by its mentality—these are maybe even crazier, stranger, and even more unprecedented things than if a tree or a mountain shifted position merely by the power of the human word. If we have never had the feeling that what Jesus wants of us is absurd, crazy, and impossible, then we've probably either been too hasty in taming or diluting the radical nature of his teaching by means of soothing intellectualizing interpretations, or (mostly naïvely, illusorily, or even hypocritically) we have too easily forgotten just to what extent—in our thinking, customs, and actions—we are rooted "in this world" where totally different rules apply.

When reality was separated into the "objective" and the "subjective" at the beginning of the modern era, God was made homeless. Any attempt to place Him into one or another of the categories always resulted in "the death of God." God did not belong in the world of things, the world of visible, measurable, provable, and, above all, manipulable "realities." But nor is God a "feeling," a "thought," or an "idea," even if human thoughts and feelings can become attached to Him (until they eventually discover that not even they can penetrate His mystery, and at best they can just about touch the "hem of his garment").

"My Kingdom does not belong to this world."[6] God's place is in the "kingdom of the impossible," in the "kingdom of absurdity," somewhere where a totally different logic applies than in "this world"—the logic of the paradox: if you want to be bigger, then be the least, be the servant of all; whoever loses his life will gain it; those who have will receive, while from those who have not, even what they have will be taken away; the laborer hired for the last hour will receive the same wage as the one that has "borne the day's burden and the heat"; the master from whom the "dishonest steward" has stolen, praises him for acting prudently; the father shows more feeling toward the prodigal son than toward the son who has been faithful and obedient; the Son of the Most High is born in a stable and executed on a cross among felons; the dead come to life, the blind see, and those who say "we see" have become blind.

Is that any basis for some system, logic, or morality, for some rational, healthy, and successful "lifestyle"? It's impossible. Viewed "from here" it is the "kingdom of the impossible." "For human beings it is impossible," Jesus often enjoyed saying, "but for God all things are possible."[7] "Nothing is impossible for God."[8] What is impossible for humans is possible for God—and we can see God only in "what is impossible for people." People's attempts to penetrate the mystery of God's essence inevitably go astray; maybe there is only one path where we might conceivably encounter the ever astonishing *kingdom of the impossible* that is coming. That path is the *path of paradox.*

However, the mustard seed conceals within it the dynamic of growth. In another parable in which Jesus compares the mustard seed to the kingdom of heaven, he again points to the paradox of the large and small—from smallest beginnings, from a tiny seed, "the smallest of all the seeds," there grows a mighty tree on whose branches birds come and perch.[9] Living faith has a similar dynamic: it includes the courage to trust, to open oneself up, to transcend "mental barriers"—to act and hope, to hope and act. In contrast to all the caricatures of faith that we have mentioned, this is not a power that manipulates us or seeks to manipulate the reality around us. We must not use this power for our own benefit or to achieve greater performance, or to win people's admiration.

The "impossible things" that are the expression of faith and whereby that "kingdom of the impossible" enters our lives (and the world also), such as forgiveness, nonviolence, and generous, unselfish love—generally bring the opposite of success. That is something that is also evident from Jesus's life story: his "downward career."

Trust and unselfish love can truly cause us problems and even have sad and often traumatizing consequences. "Following Jesus" and implementing in this world the logic of the "kingdom of the impossible" requires courage (foolishness in the world's eyes); sometimes one is even obliged to *act contrary to one's experience*. In that respect faith is truly "super-empirical" and "extra-empirical"—not because it has anything to do with ghost stories, but because it teaches us to go beyond our traumatizing *experiences* of the world of selfishness and violence.

"This world," in which the "law of the most powerful" applies and in which inconsiderateness and sharp elbows are the rule, offers only three options to those who don't like it: despair and become resigned, adapt and "do as the Romans do," or lull and benumb your senses with some drug or other. After all, there are innumerable drugs on the market from the chemical kind to the religious ones!

Faith means the courage to *opt for a fourth possibility*: to persevere on the path of unselfishness, nonviolence, and generous love, even if it means defying this world's logic, power, and usual style. The apostle Paul repeatedly describes this conflict as a dispute between "the spirit" (*pneuma*) and the "body" or "flesh" (*sarx*), and he acknowledges that this struggle has been hard for him, and that he frequently would have been defeated or given up had he not been supported by the power of God. But that power—yet another typical paradox of Paul's—is most clearly displayed in human weakness.[10]

Jesus clearly states that those who decide to *follow in his footsteps* must not be under any illusion that it is the wide, comfortable path chosen by the majority, or that its difficulties might "pay off" and lead to success in this world. The repeated references to the cross remind us to be very realistic in our expectations, that is, to count on adversities and fiascos of every kind, and have the courage to accept sacrifice, sometimes even the supreme sacrifice. And yet that "fourth way" makes sense.

This fourth way is the "fourth dimension of reality." It is the sphere "in which God dwells." From the human viewpoint it is a "realm of the impossible," of that which does not suit "this world" and cannot enter it.

Seen from the other side, from the viewpoint of faith, God is what makes sense of "absurd" and "irrational" behavior such as unselfishness and nonviolence. He makes sense of it but doesn't give any guarantee of success—let us not confuse the two! "If we count on God," then, and only then, does the "path of Jesus" and following Jesus make sense.

The significance of a life journey that strives for the *impossible*, for unselfish love, is not to be found "in the world." That, too, is why it is beyond the power, scope, or means of this world to demonstrate or verify it. For "this world" and its logic it remains absurd.[11]

Throughout our lives we have traumatic experiences of various kinds of evil, as well as of the transience of ourselves and the world, and, eventually, of death. *If we believe* in a "good God" and "eternal life," this faith is a form of defiance in the face of our own traumatic experience—I believe "in spite of all," "nonetheless." Tertullian is reputed to have said: "I believe because it is absurd."

Only two paths lead to the realization that selfless, sacrificial love makes sense: "faith" and "hope." They both have one basic thing in common: they transcend the horizon of "the possible," of what is usual and expected. They have the character of a gift. In terms of traditional theology, faith and hope, in common with love, are "infused" divine virtues; they are the fruit of grace, a gift freely given as an expression of God's *unconditional* love.

That love *precedes* our own. Moreover, it can also be a gradual corrective—as a "contrasting experience"—to our own previous traumatic experiences with our failing love. Human love endures so many internal wounds as it is confronted now with the world's harshness, now with our own limits, now with our weaknesses and our own failures, until eventually it is confronted with the boundary of the human world, which is death!

In *this world*, confronted by everything that tries to foist upon us a cynical attitude to life, our faith assumes "merely" the form of *hope*. Can one really link something like hope with the word "merely"? After all, hope is that colossal force that refuses to give up and says "nonetheless" and "once more."

When Jesus first came to Simon, the apostle Peter to be, he found him amid a group of fishermen, frustrated by a night's fruitless fishing.[12] Jesus offers them hope at the point when their own hopes, notions, and expectations—based on their own experience—had reached their limit and they had given up. "We have worked hard all night and have caught nothing." But Peter's faith is born out of his courage to trust, to trust in the impossible: "*but at your command* I will lower the nets." His entire faith is contained in that little word "but," the trust that expresses itself in his courage to try "once more."

This scene of the first meeting between Peter and Jesus corresponds to the scene of their last meeting, at the selfsame spot: on that occasion, after his traumatic experience with this disciple, who is by turns exceedingly zealous and woefully fallible, Jesus gives Peter, after his latest and worst lapse—the triple denial—"another chance."

We have spoken about the path of love as being an "absurdity" in the eyes of "this world's logic." But let us recall the many occasions on which, on the contrary, "this world," the world of our mounting experience of violence and malice, has seemed absurd and meaningless.

One of the most remarkable currents in our Western culture—one encompassing the existential philosophers from Kierkegaard to Sartre or Camus and literature and drama from Dostoyevsky and Franz Kafka to the "absurd theater" of Ionesco and Beckett—is an obvious expression of that "mood of the the age." Over the past two centuries, how many people have been tempted, like Ivan Karamazov, "to return God" their ticket into this senselessly cruel world?!

However, the very fact of protest against the world's cruelty, the fact that people find such a world absurd, proves that human beings yearn for meaning. Insofar as people are human they are incapable of calmly accepting evil and hopelessness. They do not give up, but long to evade this world's condition. Yet the world's condition does not itself open for them any "door to meaning."

If love, faith, and hope seem absurd according to the "logic of this world," while from the perspective of the human heart that yearns and suffers "this world" appears absurd, it means that there is something in the human heart that fundamentally gravitates toward sense and meaning "in spite of everything," "nonetheless." There is something in the heart that is open to meaning (or at least the possibility of meaning) in protest, yearning, and hope.

Can we believe that, for its part, the realm of meaning is open to the human heart and its call? There is nothing in this world or this life to provide us with a clear and irrefutable answer to that question. Our entire personal experience, our rationality and imagination are all too immersed in this world and hemmed in by its limits. Yet again "only" through faith and hope can we be receptive to the possibility of a positive answer. There is no other way to transcend the barrier of the absurdity of our world and of everything "in it," including death. Nevertheless, this is precisely a situation in which Christ's words also resonate, when he says: "For human beings this is impossible, but for God all things are possible."[13]

And so I would also like to conclude this meditation with a petition: Your Kingdom come! Let it come and let us enter the place where what seems impossible to us becomes possible. Let us enter the place where the possibilities that You open up—when we have exhausted all of our own ones—make it *possible* for us, in spite of everything, to persevere and remain faithful to You in this impossible world of ours!

. 4 .

Intimation of the Presence

Adoro te devote, latens Deitas—I adore you devoutly, O Godhead unseen. During these quiet weeks in the hermitage these words at the beginning of the hymn about the Eucharist have become a kind of *mantra*—a prayer rhythmically repeated over and over again. As every year, the Eucharist is displayed day and night in a small monstrance on the altar table in the corner of my room. I look at it every time I raise my eyes from the text I am reading or writing, or from any other activity. I spend the time set aside for prayer and meditation in front of it, and sometimes I sit in front of it in the middle of the night. Ever since my conversion, quiet lingering in contemplation before the exposed Eucharist has been for me the thing that is most congenial and precious from the treasury of traditional Catholic spirituality.

This year, however, the "adoration of the unseen God" also became the central theme of my reflections during my spiritual exercises whose "by-product" is this book. And so these opening words of the Eucharistic hymn form also a kind of bridge between my prayer and my work, in accordance with the principle bequeathed to the monks and hermits of all time by Saint Benedict: *Ora et labora!*

The white Host recalls one of the key paschal metaphors: Jesus as bread given into the hands of people. At the same time, this Eucharistic self-distribution of Christ is the culmination of the mystery that we celebrate at Easter: Christ's humanity has the paradoxical character of a symbol—it discloses and conceals at one and the same time; it brings the *godhead* nearer by revealing it to our senses, but it becomes a "stumbling block" for those who are unwilling to see or understand.

In front of the Eucharist I often recall Teilhard de Chardin's mystical text about the sacrament of the altar as the glowing hearth of divine *dynamis*, which shines through matter and makes the whole of creation transparent vis-à-vis its Creator. The Eucharist is a place, an "event," where the *fruit of the earth* (representing the entire cosmos, the whole of nature and matter) and *the fruit of human labor* (representing the whole of human culture) encounter God's design of permeating the whole of reality through the Incarnation and through the self-emptying of Christ (*kenosis*) and changing it from its foundations through His presence. The apostle Paul perceived the entire drama of creation as a single surge of longing. He felt in the pulse of nature a trembling anticipation, the great advent, the eager waiting "for the sons of God to be revealed." For Paul all the pains of the world were simply the birth pangs of a "new creation." Similarly in his "Mass on the World" in the Ordos Desert, Teilhard is conscious of placing on the paten all the power hidden within human aspirations, activity, and yearning, and into the chalice all human "accepted passivity," pain, and suffering—and all this must be *transformed*.

Whenever I read and meditate upon Teilhard's reflections

on the Eucharist, I ask myself how it was possible that a priest
who understood and felt this specific mystery of the innermost
sanctuary of Catholic spirituality with such depth and sensitivity could be regarded by some with such animosity and blind-
ness as a "pagan" or "heretic." Or is the fact that within "God's
family" there remain shadows of tensions, misunderstandings,
and conflicts also part of the finiteness of humanity that God
took upon Himself to *hide* therein "the light of His face"?

During the past academic year I have reminded my students,
among other things, of four leading Christian thinkers of the
century that recently ended, and whose jubilees occurred last
year or this. I felt that the four of them could help illustrate
the great breadth and plurality of Christianity in our times.
Whereas Teilhard de Chardin (d. 1955) was interested in the
sacred, white-hot energy of the *"milieu divin"*[1] (the divine environment) that permeated the entire universe down to the very
last speck of matter, Dietrich Bonhoeffer (d. 1945) advocated a
"religionless Christianity" and faith's radical approval of the secular world without religious crutches. The two greatest Catholic
theologians of the twentieth century from the German-speaking
world, Karl Rahner and Hans Urs von Balthasar, the centen-
nials of whose births have occurred over these past two years,
certainly resembled each other to a degree, including the fact
that prior to the Second Vatican Council these two pioneers of
a more dynamic and profound reflection on faith than that of
the prevailing neo-scholasticism encountered distrust and ha-
rassment of every kind from within the Church. But eventually
their paths diverged: Rahner became a kind of living symbol of
the intellectual renewal of Catholic Christianity after Vatican II,
while Urs von Balthasar was sharply critical of much of that development (and also of Rahner). Their subsequent careers were
also very different. After leaving the Jesuit order in the 1950s,

Urs von Balthasar spent years trying to find a bishop prepared to accept him into his diocese and allow him to say Mass publicly, and then, just days before his death, he was appointed cardinal by Pope John Paul II; Rahner, on the other hand, or so the story goes, did not find much favor with that same pope.

As I "sort out my ideas" a bit, as well as my lecture notes, it strikes me that these four very different thinkers, each of them from a different angle, profoundly elucidate the theme that has caught my imagination so strongly here: the theme of *God's hiddenness*.

The Jesuit Teilhard and the Protestant pastor Bonhoeffer, who most likely never heard of each other or read each other's writings, articulated around the same time their ideas about how to heal Christianity and the civilization of their day, which they both perceived to be in a state of serious disorder.

They both underwent firsthand the most drastic experience of the twentieth century—world war. It was as a frontline medical orderly in World War I that Teilhard experienced his key mystic vision of humanity coalescing into one, while Bonhoeffer set out in letters his vision for a "Christianity without religion" just before he was executed at the very end of World War II for his part in the anti-Nazi resistance.

Teilhard's diagnosis ran as follows: at the start of the twentieth century Christianity was "underhumanized." Christianity, which had once been capable of inspiring powerful spiritual currents, was now timorous and turned inward, incapable of absorbing new values. In particular, it displayed a lack of understanding for modern humanism, for the aspirations of a new awareness; it failed to respond to contemporary people's religious enthusiasm, and as a result people were seeking different paths because Christianity had ceased to be "infectious." Christianity had ceased to be a common ideal of humankind and had become sterile—because it *failed to love the world enough*. Its teaching and spiritual practice had been crippled by the old heresies—Manichaean dualism that rejected matter and creation, and Jansenism with its pessimistic attitude to natural human behavior, its pathological asceticism, and its obsession with original sin. The contemporary form of Christianity displayed an inadequate awareness of the *dynamism* of both God and the world; its understanding of the universe was too static—which was one of the reasons that it had a rigid view of God and a too-narrow, *private* concept of salvation: it was not enough to be concerned solely with the salvation of individual "souls," because God promised much more: the overall transformation of earth and heaven.

Teilhard's personality and thinking display many of the typical charismata of the Jesuit order: characteristically wide-ranging scholarship, refinement and generosity, as well as a clairvoyant ability to read the signs of the times and respond to them promptly, not to mention the courage to take risks in places most in danger. Teilhard devoted his life to the natural sciences, and not only did he achieve outstanding results in that field with his attempt at an original spiritual and theological interpretation of the then prevalent understanding of the universe based chiefly on evolutionism, but he also considered it part and parcel of his vocation to show profound spiritual solidarity with the international scientific community within which he worked.

Indeed he regarded the efforts of scientists to be the profoundest spiritual impulse of the times. He insisted on the greatest possible interconnection between centers of scientific rationality. Unlike most of the theologians of the day, he did not reject the values that were then current—radical humanism, the theory of evolution, belief in progress, even in social progress based on rationality, technology, and science. He wanted to take those values *even more seriously than they were taken by their secular advocates.* He tried passionately to penetrate the very core of those endeavors, because he regarded them as a response to God's challenge; he sensed in them the courage to acknowledge the *élan vital* that God Himself had placed in His creation. He was not discouraged or disconcerted at all by the fact that the scientists he worked and talked with about these matters largely espoused atheism, agnosticism, positivism, Darwinism, or Marxism. He was convinced that "today's materialists are spiritualists who are unaware of the fact," and that the contemporary world was by no means cool toward religion; on the contrary it was *fervid.* And if that spiritual fervor assumed a different form and called itself something other than "Christianity," then it was the fault of Christians themselves, and they should take up the challenge of that reality.

Teilhard de Chardin might be described as the first philosopher of *globalization,* although he never used the term. The vision of a *planetary unification of humankind* increasingly became central to his thinking.

Whereas the conservative critique of scientific and technological civilization drew attention to its pitfalls and dangers, Teilhard tried all the harder to argue in favor of its prospects. He maintained that automation could encourage creative thinking and that the mass media could extend the opportunity to see many things, and thereby help arouse more compassion and solidarity, as well as the capacity for mutual understanding and love. He believed that humankind was becoming *planetary* and that this irreversible process would oblige it to learn coexistence and cooperation. He believed that indestructible networks of mutual dependence were being created in the world, which would stimulate a great movement of unification. Teilhard is criticized by many for underestimating the totalitarian regimes of the twentieth century because of his passionate optimism. In his view, however, the totalitarian regimes were simply a caricature and deviant form of real unity.

Wars and conflicts arouse a yearning for better unification, Teilhard maintained; after all, that yearning was always expressed with greatest fervor after wars and revolutions. Shortly humanity would create a single bloc; what humanity was living through was simply the beginning and birth pangs of the planetary civilization of tomorrow. Humankind was still in the embryonic stage of its evolution—an "ultra-humanity" was already looming on the horizon beyond it. The essence of growth was unification: "to be" meant "to seek greater unity."

Not surprisingly, Marxists were attracted by Teilhard's vision of the future, particularly since Teilhard himself adopted a generous attitude toward them. This is because he was convinced that Marxist atheism was essentially an error due to the Marxists' rejection of what was only a caricature of God, the "deus ex machina." Naturally Teilhard's expectations of the future differed fundamentally both from the Marxist revolutionary utopia and from the naïve reliance on "self-propelled" scientific rationality espoused by the ideologists of technological progress and economic prosperity as the guarantee of happy tomorrows.

Teilhard sensed that at the present phase of civilization, at a time of unprecedentedly greater human control of natural forces, the critical moment was arriving when humanity would be faced with a major choice. Whereas until then humanity had been able to look upon evolution—from the beginnings of matter to its own civilization—as something spontaneous, it was now obliged to eschew all determinist theories; the next step could only be taken through *understanding*, on the basis of free choice. The options were pessimism, which Teilhard considered humanity's desertion and suicide; escape into an otherworldly asceticism, individualism, and egoistical separation of people's private interests; or, finally, the option that he himself considered the only real way forward: demonstrating *faithfulness to the earth*[2]—by building the future unity of humankind not as an ant heap of forced collectivization or a free market of individual competing interests, but as a *personalist* community.

Love is the only force that unifies things without destroying them. The Christian community has a fundamental role in this—to bear witness by developing the principle of love; no other force, Teilhard repeats, can complete the process of universal convergence.

At this point, Teilhard's *hidden God* comes into play—by the fact that the *alpha* and *omega*, the starting point of transcendence and the final goal and summit of the convergence of the entire evolutionary process of the universe, is God. It is God and Jesus Christ, who is God's creative Word, who was at the beginning and will be at the end; he is *Christus evolutor,* incarnate in the world, in the material and historical universe, and present here through the community of believers, woven into humanity. It is he, the mysterious and often unrecognized Christ, who introduces into the historical movement of human society the lasting central force that humanity must experience if it is to achieve final fulfillment.

Today, half a century after Teilhard's death, in our *post-optimistic age*, the pathos of his visions may seem to many worthy of no more than being shelved—with appropriate irony and skepticism—along with many "great narratives," myths, and naïvely optimistic philosophies of progress from the nineteenth century, and their posthumous ideological progeny of the subsequent century. But we should bear in mind that Teilhard was no magician, effortlessly producing promises of radiant tomorrows like so many authors in the Enlightenment tradition. The source of Teilhard's visions—as Jan Patočka recalls in his last and most mature work, the *Heretical Essays in the Philosophy of*

History—were his appalling experiences at the front in World War I.[3] It was in that bloody slaughterhouse, in the dark forge of suffering and death, in which it was impossible to distinguish between "ours" and "theirs," that he saw a sort of smelting pot of experience that Patočka described as the "solidarity of the shaken," a realization that we all share the same fate, the same peril, the same anxieties—and therefore we must unite in our hope, also.

Likewise, Pastor Bonhoeffer's reflections on the future and role of Christianity did not germinate in the comfort of a university study, but in the *valley of the shadow of death*—in a prison cell in the shadow of the gallows.

Bonhoeffer gradually shifted from his earlier notions of "moral renewal of the West" to a much harsher critique of embourgeoised Christianity. Self-centered and isolated from the surrounding world, the Church was no longer capable of being a vehicle for the healing message of reconciliation and redemption. It was necessary to go out into the fresh air of coming to terms with the world; it was necessary to speak a new language.

Even the key concept of religion—"God"—had become so worn and shabby that it was necessary to *do without it*. Not *without God*, but without the concept of God as a hypothesis to explain the mysteries of the world; without the god that we use to fill the dark corners still unexplored by scientific rationality; without the penalizing god that preachers can use to terrify and blackmail their flocks; without "the powerful god of religion" onto whom we can foist our own responsibility and who tranquilizes us in our passivity toward evil, in our bourgeois coziness and social conformity.

Bonhoeffer the theologian welcomed the modern critique of religion and agreed with it; he welcomed rationalism and demanded intellectual honesty from Christians: it was impossible to ignore the fact that the "metaphysical preconditions for God" and for the previous understanding of God had been destroyed, in the same way that circumcision and many other obligations of the Mosaic law had been done away with by the faith of Christians, thanks to Paul's efforts. *Before God and with God we live without God*—so runs Bonhoeffer's paradoxical statement, and it is not by chance that it recalls the German mystics, that important, though often neglected source of Luther's Reformation theology.

Bonhoeffer's prophetic fervor chiefly focuses on demolishing models, which is one reason that it differs greatly from Teilhard's poetical prophetism of hope in growing cosmic unification. Nevertheless, in spite of all the dissimilarity—particularly their different *style* of thinking and expression—I find surprising points of congruence between them. Both refer to "faithfulness to the earth"; both are sympathetic to secular people's humanism; they both recognize and support the rationality and "maturity" of the civilization of their time; they both stress the need to live in a secular world without escaping into an "otherworld." They realize that it is necessary to bear witness to Christian belief in transcendence *by living that transcendence in the world*; Christian belief in transcendence must be attested to by (living) transcendence in the world—*by effectual love and solidarity*, and by overcoming the temptation to selfishness and indolence. Both reject "religious alibis" for indifference to the fate of people in the world around us.

Teilhard's God *hidden* within the power of matter, in the earthly longings of the human heart, and in the creative élan of the universe is not "incompatible" with the *hiddenness of God* in Bonhoeffer's gospel of secular Christianity. For both of them the central point is God, even though they look at God from different perspectives. According to Teilhard, God made Christ the alpha and the omega, the initial source and final objective of the evolution of the entire cosmos. Bonhoeffer maintains that the world and the life therein have meaning only because Christ lived in this world. The God of Bonhoeffer's faith is present in the world solely in Jesus's self-sacrificing humanity—as well as in the undemonstrative witness of his followers, in their *being for others,* in their freedom from themselves; in following Christ to the death if necessary. In the view of Pastor Bonhoeffer, Christian faith is not a religious conviction but a participation in Christ's *Being*; it is a *new life for others.*

Bonhoeffer, who must have come to know, particularly in prison, many of those who, out of human solidarity and for the cause of freedom and justice for all, were prepared to risk and sacrifice their own lives, even though they had not embarked on that path consciously inspired by the example of Jesus and "for his name's sake," would certainly not have begrudged such people the status of (unconscious but real) kinship and affiliation with Christ: a kinship for which the next of the thinkers I want to mention coined the term "anonymous Christians." Moreover, Teilhard also declared that he regarded "many of those who think they are on the outside" as true brothers of Christ, who are in reality closer to Christ than those who, in words but not in deeds, call him with excessive zeal "Lord, Lord."

In his extensive writings the Jesuit Karl Rahner also referred on several occasions and in various contexts to the *hiddenness of God.* Rahner was very well aware (and he splendidly articulated it in one of his last texts, which can be read as a kind of intellectual testament—his bequest to theologians) that theological discourse about God must always be inspired by the tradition of *negative theology.* And it ought to be ready to accept its corrective influence whenever it is tempted to forget that it operates solely in the field of analogical and metaphorical speech, whenever it is tempted to cross glibly the threshold of the inaccessible light of mystery and slide into shallow ideology or banality. I want to mention only one theme of Rahner's theology, which is closely and interestingly related to the idea of God's hiddenness, namely, Rahner's frequently cited theory of *anonymous Christianity.*

Just as in the case of Teilhard's concept of God's presence in the powers of the universe, so also in Rahner's theory of anonymous Christianity it is a God working through Jesus Christ, not some fuzzy pantheistic or deistic concept of the "godhood." His entire theory, in fact, is directly based on an original and bold extrapolation of Christian teaching about the Incarnation.

God's Word took upon itself human nature; the German expression *Menschwerdung* indicates that it is something dynamic, more of a "process"—the act of becoming man. In Rahner's view, the most authentic human response to "God's becoming man" (*Menschwerdung Gottes*) is *man becoming man* (*Menschwerdung des Menschen*).

Our human existence is not something static, an accomplished fact; every moment—and particularly at moments of major moral decision—our humanity is in formation. Those who accept and bear their human lot conscientiously, with patient awareness that it is bounded and finite, who constantly seek meaning, particularly in love toward and solidarity with others, also connect with the mystery of the Incarnation through that existential acceptance of their humanity, even if they have never heard of the Incarnation or concurred with it by an explicit act of faith.

And because Christian faith, as we have said on many occasions already, is not a mere "conviction," the espousal of certain opinions, but is *people's existential participation in the life of God* by following Christ, we can hope that this participation stems from an authentic human life and anticipates (and possibly implicitly consists of) explicit agreement with and assertion of that mysterious linkage of human life and the life of God. Because those who have not come to know Christ or have not encountered him in a way that would allow them to sincerely accept him subjectively—assuming that they do not explicitly and freely reject him—are *in their conscientious humanity* "on the same boat" as the community of Christ's followers. Christians can hope for the salvation of such people, even if "through no fault of their own" they are not baptized and are considered (or consider themselves) "nonbelievers" in the Christian sense of the word, or are devotees of other religions. We can call them "anonymous Christians": they are *with us*; they belong to us without knowing it. Moreover, Jesus himself said: "Who is not against us, is with us," and in his description of the Last Judgment he hints that those who will take a seat at his right hand because they have shown love to the needy will be surprised that he was present in the suffering, because they clearly did not belong to his visible family of devotees on earth, who called him "Lord, Lord."

Rahner's teaching about "anonymous Christians" was a significant corrective to the widespread understanding of the sentence "outside the Church there is no salvation."[4] It clearly also influenced the historic declaration of the Second Vatican Council about the possibility of salvation of the non-baptized and those believers of other faiths—a position still little known to many Catholics, or at least not "well digested." It also created a significant, albeit by now largely obsolete, theological basis for the Catholic determination to develop interreligious dialogue and cooperation.

Yet again the *hidden God* is evident—the God whom we must seek and find in the lives of people beyond the visible boundaries of the Church.

.   .   .

There are also many reflections on *God's hiddenness* to be found in the writings of Hans Urs von Balthasar, the Swiss Catholic theologian who has been described as possibly the most erudite person of the twentieth century. A powerful source of inspiration for his thinking were the Greek patristic texts—a tradition that is permeated with the theme of a hidden God, *dwelling in inaccessible light*; it is a theme that emerges directly from the heart of the entire theology and spirituality of the Christian East.

Likewise, Urs von Balthasar, albeit more cautiously than Rahner, speaks in terms of a certain "anonymous form" of relationship with the hidden God, present not only in all religions, but also in atheistic humanism. He believes that evidence of a *certain awe in the face of the mystery of being*, including a willingness to speak about this hidden mystery, can also be found in "the humanitarian world views which today describe themselves as religionless," which "draw their strength, at least in the cases where they do not publicly proclaim their cynicism and demonism, from a primal pathos. They have been gripped by a sense of the urgency of the task of reconciling man with the universal being of the world; hungering and thirsting after ultimate righteousness are not possible without a sense of awe in the face of the mystery of being."[5]

And in his essay on the necessity of contemplation Urs von Balthasar also talks about the solidarity of believers with nonbelievers.

> Could any Christian want to pray merely for himself, without including his brothers who do not pray, in his prayer before God? . . . Such a man will pray out of gratitude to God and out of responsibility for his fellow men. He will not pay a great deal of attention to his own feelings or lack of

feelings, to the extent to which he experiences God's presence or absence. Perhaps *he will be allowed to feel the absent
God of those who do not pray, in order that the latter may
catch an intimation of the God who is present.* Such things
are given within the *communio sanctorum*, which in the
widest sense is the community of all those for whom God
on the Cross has borne and suffered total abandonment.
And that indeed is everyone.[6]

The evening has advanced, here in the hermitage, the time
has come in the regular rhythm of my days for my moments of
contemplation at the day's end. These moments of the evening
are also my ministry of "spiritual solidarity" with those who are
far away—not just physically, but also spiritually. At those moments may I pray for at a least an "intimation of the presence"
for one of those for whom God remains utterly hidden and who
do not call God by name?

I am mutely aware of the white silence of the Host, displayed
on the simple monstrance on the massive oak table. The Eucharist, Saint Thomas Aquinas teaches, embraces all three dimensions of time. It is a memorial or remembrance (*anamnesis*) of
Christ's submission to death (*memoria mortis Domini*), a potent
sign of his hidden presence here and now, and a "foretaste" of
the banquet in the Kingdom of his future.

I do nothing, say nothing, and think about nothing. I simply
breathe, as I was taught by an Indian Jesuit: breathing out to
surrender all my cares, anxieties, and sadness; breathing in to
draw in his peace, joy, and strength. Just as when waves crash
into a rock and then return to the sea, so also can the human
being, in this rhythm of inhalation and exhalation, almost physically experience what was expressed by Paul the apostle: "for
when I am weak, then I am strong."[7] But it is not simply related to myself—*no man is an island.* The cares, wounds, and

weaknesses of my church are also *my* weaknesses; the sadness and darkness of those who lack the awareness of God's nearness are also my chasms. But the outgoing tide rhythmically gives way to the incoming tide, and with it one can feel—or at least sense—the waves of peace, strength, and joy: *For rejoicing in the Lord*, says Scripture, *must be your strength.*[8]

. 5 .

Discreet Faith

"No, I'm sorry, I really won't come," I respond apologetically to the two youngsters who have come to invite me to some mega-rally of young Christians, organized by two of the present "new movements" in the Catholic Church. "Youthful enthusiasm for Christ" organized on a mass scale, with "Hi there, brothers and sisters" from the platform and arms raised and eyes popping in the audience. No, that is not "my cup of tea," as the English say. I have never felt at ease among religious enthusiasts. Some years ago, during the visit of the pope, I observed one particular "youth pastor" as, with all seriousness, he led his flock in chanting en masse a rhyming slogan that included the words "Let us all rejoice in the Lord, our Daddy's come from the Vatican— Hurrah!" My feeling at that moment was more or less the same as Joseph K's when the butcher's knife is thrust into his heart in the Strahov quarry at the end of Kafka's novel *The Trial*: I *thought the shame of it would outlive me.*

I myself came to faith slowly *through a process of doubt*; I find it hard to imagine being suddenly infected by collective piety at some mass rally with banners reading JESUS LOVES YOU and cheerleaders with unbearably fixed smiles. Besides, at the time of my conversion, stadiums and circuses still served their original purposes and were not used for religious clownery. Naturally I respect the fact that there are those who feel the need to be crushed in a crowd of like-minded people to strengthen their faith. My faith would more likely be lost in a throng like that.

A touch of skepticism, irony, and commitment to critical reason as a permanent corrective to any tendency to superficial religious enthusiasm is, in my view, not only a necessary condition for mental and spiritual health, but also a prerequisite if we are not to drown out the real voice of God with our own whooping and shouting: it reminds me of the fellow in the well-known anecdote who is looking in the dark for a black cat in a totally empty room and calling out rather prematurely: "I've got it, I've got it!"

"I'd be unpleasantly ironic there and spoil your mood," I explain to those two nice young people. "I'm simply a born skeptic, and what most likely brought me to faith was my determination to be consistent—and so I was even skeptical about my skepticism."

Shouldn't I have been more skeptical toward my skepticism about such events? I asked myself after they left in disappointment. What if covertly I actually envy the youthful simplicity of their piety, which possibly counts for more than mine in the eyes of the Lord?

I return to that question in the evening during a period of "conscience probing." Isn't there another deeper and more personal reason that these religious enthusiasts irritate me? After all, the few really close friends I have among the Czech clergy also include priests who have been sincerely involved in the "charismatic renewal movement" for years, and although we argue from time to time, I truly respect them. Likewise, some of the best and most active young people in our parish belong to that movement in one way or another. But I could say almost the same about Focolare and several other movements: there, too, I know really fine people and upstanding Christians.

Perhaps the people from this "new movement" set up a corrective mirror in which I am to recognize that my skepticism (why did I recently spend a whole evening reading Ecclesiastes with such sympathy and why has it become almost my favorite book of the Bible?) might simply be the expression of a weariness that prevents me from being more receptive to these "youthful" forms of faith and more accommodating in my assessment of them? Is this a sign of an impending "burnout syndrome," or am I simply growing old?

All right: my hunch is that the "youthful enthusiasm for Christ" at such gatherings as the one to which I was invited is simply no more than the enthusiasm that young people feel in the emotionally charged atmosphere of a group in which they find acceptance at a moment when their family surroundings start to feel constrictive and they no longer feel understood to the same degree among their schoolmates. But what's wrong with that, in the final analysis? If I were a parent of teenagers, I'd probably be fairly happy with the thought that my children go off to enthusiastically Christian events, from which they don't come home high on drugs or HIV positive; where I can be sure they won't have their heads shaved or be brainwashed as in so many extremist religious or political sects of the Right or Left; where they will not be introduced to a satanic cult of violence and negation of the entire universe. If I had political responsibility for the upbringing of the younger generation, I would also probably welcome and support such events, even if I weren't a

Christian at all. Indeed, I would be capable of coming to the commonsense conclusion that it was not at all a bad idea that someone somewhere is teaching at least part of the younger generation that not to lie and not to steal are not such bad principles, and that there is a certain difference between a handshake and coitus as an expression of a fifteen-year-old's joy at seeing someone for the second time in their lives, and not only in experiential but also in ethical terms.

Young people will have difficulty in picking this up at school, where mention of Christian ethics (and I have not noticed that our culture has come up with anything radically different or demonstrably better) sounds ludicrous coming from the lips of teachers who, by and large, ostentatiously flout such ethics in their own lives; and where, on the other hand, many believers in the teaching profession fear that if they manifest their Christian faith too obviously in their work, they might face an inquisitional court for blaspheming against the dogmas of a peculiar interpretation of liberalism, pluralism, and multiculturalism. And again, after a certain time, parents—sometimes for good—lose all authority over their adolescent offspring, because they are required to fulfill another, more thankless role. By adopting a detached, hypercritical, and conflictual attitude to their parents, pubertal children learn to seek their own path and their own responsibility. Few parents manage to cope calmly and cheerfully with the fact that almost overnight they are obliged to become a springboard, on which their own children learn—stamping painfully on them in the process—to make their first vital, albeit sometimes risky, leap into freedom.

"The good Lord knows why He made a priest out of you: because you would be an utterly unbearable and irritable father, in spite of your international Tolerance Prize" is what I hear from time to time from a woman who knows me fairly well. "You are really only tolerant toward Muslims and Sikhs because you meet them twice a year at some conference in Washington, at the Vatican, or in Brussels—as far away as possible from your own front door." She exaggerates, of course, but maybe there is a grain of truth in it, after all. What is it that really irritates me about those mass rallies, those movements of enthusiasts, and those booklets with titles like "How to Talk to Young People about God," if I detach myself from my basic antipathy toward attempts to pass off manipulated crowd fervor as "a gust of the Holy Spirit"?

Yes, of course, I also dislike such rallies on *aesthetic* grounds. I insist that the beauty of religion and manifestations of religion (including the space for worship) is not some sort of superfluous and almost dangerous "superstructure" for fastidious aesthetes. In retrospect I have found that few things prove as reliable an indicator of the health, depth, and authenticity of some community's spirituality as its sensitivity—or lack of it—to beauty, one of the traditional characteristics of God.

My religious taste was nurtured (thanks to Father Jiří Reinsberger, a follower of Saint Benedict) by the splendid symmetry of the classical Catholic liturgy, particularly the Order of the Mass (and I would not mind in the least attending *occasionally* a preconciliar Latin Mass with Gregorian chant, or even serving one, if only its proponents were not so sectarian and narrowly single-minded, and did not insist that it is the *only* proper form). I fail to understand why, at those giant rallies at stadiums, whether they be solely Catholic or ecumenical, Catholics seem unable to make greater use of that spirit of their liturgy and offer this incredible gift to those Christians who have lost that culture to their own detriment and (with all due ecumenical courtesy) have grown barren and somewhat barbarized in that respect. Why, on the contrary, do Catholics neglect that treasure, with the result that those rallies resemble what I encounter in some non-Catholic churches that strive to "be in tune with the times," and which never fail to take me aback—namely, that the chaotic structure of their services gives the impression of a crudely improvised "religious vaudeville." But that is still not my most serious objection.

What I object to most of all is the brazenly casual way that people there trumpet out the great words of our faith through loudspeakers. Yesterday evening I read about ten times over a sentence that expressed precisely what has afflicted me so dreadfully over the years: "It is the tragedy of modern Western culture to have fallen victim to the illusion (widely shared by believer and nonbeliever alike) that it is perfectly easy to talk about God."[1]

No, I don't believe the trite and oft-repeated assertion that for pedagogical reasons one must start with simplifications before gradually proceeding to more complex things. I most firmly oppose that notion, at the very least, in the fields of philosophy and religion. The moment people assent to simplification, trivialization, banalization, to the feeling that "everything is clear," it is "sickness unto death." They are most likely to end up either *dumbing down*, religiously speaking (something that has absolutely nothing in common with the simplicity of children and infants that Jesus speaks of—and it is a dreadful insult to the Gospel, children, and simple people if they are deliberately confused), or eventually rejecting all religion with contempt.

The point is that those who operate the large-scale religious simplification industry never offer that promised "next stage," because they themselves have never reached it and it is totally alien to them; whenever they encounter the "more complex" aspects of faith they think it is the work of the devil. Superficial or shallow religion leads only deeper and deeper into the mire or to the aridity of the desert, not to the depths.

Those who wish to seek the living God and truly follow

Christ must have the courage to learn to *swim in deep water*, not in the shallows. God *is* the depths; He is not to be found in the shallows.

The path of faith and "knowing God" is not learning some subject or skill, where the desired result is "mastering" the thing, and where it is best to proceed systematically—such as when learning the piano—from "Frère Jacques" to Beethoven's piano concertos. Until Christian teachers take seriously the idea that God Himself *is the depth of all reality*, and not some "subject of knowledge," many sermons and religious dissertations and courses will fail to *develop an awareness of depth* and just keep bashing out "Frère Jacques"—and that song will start to sound increasingly out of tune and unbearable.

Of course, certain specific "techniques" of spiritual life, as well as the study of theology or the traditions of the Church, not to mention getting a grounding in the world of liturgy, all require mastering by means of perseverance and a systematic step-by-step approach. But that is something else. When some-one is *introduced into the faith* they need to be told clearly that they are being introduced into *a world of mystery and depth*, that Jesus is not "a pal they can chat with," and God is not a Daddy represented by the appropriate ecclesiastical daddies, to whom we shall all now cry "hurrah," and once more "hurrah," and "Al-leluia, Lord Jesus"—"Come on, kids, you can do better than that: at the top of your voices and all together!"

Whenever I see a priest who has preserved the ingenuous charm of eternal boyhood by dint of indulging solely in this kind of piety, I don't regret growing old. Whenever I see portly daddies and venerable matrons at big stadiums weeping profusely as they sway in rhythm and shout "hurrah" and "Alleluia, Lord Jesus" with their arms in the air, it strikes me that it would be more appropriate for this undoubtedly healthy form of emotional catharsis if the stadium were being used at that moment for a splendid football match or a hard rock concert; I'm not entirely sure why our Lord has to be dragged into it.

I can't help suspecting that the enduring "substance" of such rallies is the "spirit of the stadium," while the "Holy Spirit" and the "Lord Jesus," who are invoked there through the loudspeakers, become simply one of its interchangeable options.

Unless we tell people in time that God dwells in inaccessible light, that prayer is silence for Mystery, and that faith is respecting that mystery and adjusting to it *as a mystery,* and that any shout of "I've got it" is simply proof that one has strayed from the path, then we deceive them and ourselves and there is no truth in us. The truth about God and God as the truth of our lives is always paradoxical. It is within us only if we do not try to "hold on to it" and triumphantly own it.

"I've had enough of your talk about God's hiddenness, unfathomable mystery, and silence. After all, wasn't God revealed? Did He not speak with His entire authority and commitment? Don't we have Revelation, Scripture, Christ, the Church, its sacraments, dogmas, and magisterium? Shouldn't we be expounding that to people above all and not be muddling their heads with mysticism and negative theology?"

Yes, dear brother, it is my duty to talk about these things, too. May God be witness to the kind of faith I have in Him. I don't believe in "something above us." I don't believe in the Enlightenment's god of reason, its "Supreme Being." I don't believe in the deists' "Great Watchmaker." I don't believe in the ancient Greeks' immutable Fate or the Muslims' kismet. I don't believe in the Gaia goddess or Mother Nature and her objective laws. I don't believe in the law of karma and the cycle of birth and rebirth. I don't believe in a private god, who would be an utterly private light of my conscience and my heart. I don't believe in a romantic god that would offer itself solely as a "religious sense" or *"the starry heavens above me and the moral law within me."* I strive to understand everything that those images were trying to convey, but they are not in the least the subject of my faith.

I believe in the Holy Trinity, Father, Son, and Holy Spirit—and in nothing else either in heaven or on earth. My faith is not "universal" in the sense of postmodern wishy-washiness; it does not soar free as a bird above the orchard of world religions, tasting a bit of this and a bit of that. In spite of all my willingness to listen carefully and engage in dialogue with all and sundry, my faith is *universal* in only one sense—the one that was applied to it by the early fathers of the Church and their celebrated councils: that is, it is *catholic*. It is deeply rooted in tradition and has broadly spreading branches like the mighty oak just a short distance from my hermitage.

I have no "special" personal revelation or illumination at my disposal, no "exceptional charisma" has fallen upon me in some stadium or other; I have no "special vision" that would authorize me to add anything to that faith or take anything away from it, although I do make an effort to find unhackneyed language and a fresher style with which to express it. And if certain things become evident to me slightly sooner than they do to most people, there is nothing "supernatural" about it and no reason for me to boast about it. In view of all the things I have been granted to live through, read, see, hear, reflect on, and pray about and over during the past half century, it would, on the contrary, be "unnatural," strange, and shameful if this were not the case, if all this had failed to bear any fruit at all.

My faith is ordinary: a universal, catholic, Christian faith—and I would not exchange it for any other. It is by no means the "best of a bad job" due to the lack of other goods "on offer." Allow me to paraphrase the words of the apostle: if anyone can say that they have made a thorough, extensive, and careful search of the enormous forest of world religions, then I can too. And yet I have never felt any really strong temptation to abandon Christ and the Church and exchange my faith for another. That is my confession of faith. I stand by it and "I will die with gladness" in it.

When I say "I believe in God," I know—and I offer the analyses of Augustine and many other theologians down to our own days as corroboration—that it amounts to far more than a declaration of my personal "opinions about God." The first words of the Creed in Greek and Latin, the father and mother tongues of the Church, if they were translated precisely, would say "I believe *unto* God." It is a direction indicator—it points the way, it implies movement: I believe and *my belief draws me into the Mystery* that is called God.

But how could I enter if the way was not open for me? How could I approach the Fire and not lose my way in the dazzling light, if He did not come forward to meet me? Yes, the Triune God has revealed Himself; He gives Himself and opens Himself. At the same time, however, He remains *fundamentally* incomprehensible, and it is "impossible" for all my natural capacities to recognize and see Him in this life "face-to-face."

But there are three realities through which I can contemplate Him "as if in a mirror"—and here my confession becomes truly personal, namely, a statement of my many years of experience of seeking and my faith journey. Those realities are the world, the life of Jesus, and the Church: the world, everything that is not God; Jesus's humanity and, in the light thereof, the humanity of every human being; the Church with all its riches, consisting of Scripture and tradition, the saints and the sacraments, the pope and our "separated brothers"—the Church about which Paul Evdokimov has said: "We know where the church is; it is not for us to judge and say where the Church is not."

The world reveals to me God the Creator, the Father; the

humanity of Jesus reveals to me the eternal Word of the Father, the Redeemer, the Son; the Church reveals to me *the Spirit*. In those three realities the Trinity is revealed to me; it mirrors the interpenetration (*perikhoresis*) of the "persons," but also their noninterchangeability: after all, Jesus's humanity means that he is firmly rooted in the world and its history (while, at the same time, transcending it); the Church, for its part, "grows out of Christ" and is a kind of "mystical extension" of his humanity. And yet the Church can equally be regarded as part of the world and history, albeit "unfinished" in the world, open to an eschatological future, in the same way that the end of Jesus's terrestrial story (through the "empty tomb") remains open to an eschatological completion, that is, the mystery of the Resurrection and *parousia*—the "Second Coming" of Christ.

But after professing these three realities, in which the (inaccessible) mystery of the Trinity is revealed, I must immediately add that *in this revelation also, God remains for me hidden in paradoxes*.

After all, is the world not full of tragedies that obscure the face of God for so many people and prevent them from believing in His goodness and love, and that He is all-powerful and just? Doesn't the story of Christ on earth end in the tragedy of the cross—viewed from the standpoint of the world—a tragedy that warns off and dissuades anyone who might consider following the same path? Do not the Church and its history—in the world's view full of shameful deeds and crimes, as well as the Church's pathetic presence—constitute altogether one major argument against a faith governed, cherished, and filled by the spirit of God?

"From the world's viewpoint," these objections are understandable and justified, and God possibly allowed the "worldliness" of the world (in which, of course, our own place, our own standpoint is located) precisely in order to hide Himself even more deeply against the danger of a superficial "I've got it!"

But at the same time God assigned us an odd location: "on the edge." He gave freedom of choice—including the choice of the angle from which to see and assess things. He gives us the gifts of faith and hope—not as objects "to keep" but as a light in a space that is otherwise darkened, thus offering us the possibility to view reality not only from our one single "worldly" perspective, but also from His angle, so to speak.

The world we inhabit is profoundly ambivalent and truly offers scope for both interpretations—the atheistic one and that of believers—and God will not take away from us the freedom and responsibility that are bound up with our choice.

Faith is the possibility of re-interpreting what seemed so cut and dried from "the world's" point of view. Only in the light of faith and hope can we see at the same time God's good work, and hear, in addition to all the lamentations and the cacophony of human malice and violence, God's "and it was good," which was said at the beginning and will sound at the end.

Only in the light of faith and hope can we not simply interpret Jesus's story as a story of suffering and failure, but also be enabled to hear behind "My God, why have you forsaken me?" the quiet afterword: "I have conquered the world," and "I am with you till the end of time."

Only in the light of faith and hope can we see His presence and the renewing and healing breath of the Spirit that never stops blowing—even in that often murky stream of scandals and human weakness that we call the history of the Church—the Spirit that Jesus breathed into the apostles when they were locked inside their fears, giving them the opportunity to leave their sins behind and experience his forgiveness over and over again.

But because this light, this standpoint, is not *our own*, but a real gift—like the light from Mount Tabor, where the apostles were told that they could not dwell in that light, that they could not "pitch three tents" in the sunlight of eschatological certainties[2]—our lives are in constant balance between those two points of view. There are moments when, in common with all the rebels and notorious skeptics, as well as with the sad and vainly seeking, our view of the world, Jesus, and the Church is occluded by every possible doubt or objection. But then there are moments when light breaks through the clouds and we are able—nay, we are obliged and duty-bound—to say to those rebels, skeptics, and weepers within and around us that *maybe, in spite of everything,* there is another way of seeing, assessing, and enduring all these things.

Martin Buber liked telling a story about a learned and "enlightened" teacher with books full of "overwhelming" arguments against God and belief, who came to urge his rabbi to read them. When he made a subsequent visit to the rabbi, he expected that the old man would either have capitulated in the face of his arguments and abandoned his faith, or would defend that faith tooth and nail. Instead, the rabbi weighed in his hands the man's books, heavy with all the arguments against faith that reason and human experience could muster. Then he gently stroked his Torah and, gazing at it, he simply said: *"Perhaps* it is true after all," and that terrible "perhaps" finally shook the teacher's confident atheism.

My dear young friends, maybe I'll accept your invitation one day, after all. But will *you* be able to bear having me with you when I am unable to experience God's closeness in the jubilation, the slogans, and the upraised arms, but only in that chaste "perhaps," in that "small faith"? That "perhaps" is not an expression of my lack of trust in God, but a lack of trust in myself. My concern is that our too big, too noisy, and too human certainties are in danger of obscuring what is truly great: *the Mystery*, which likes to *speak through its silence and reveal itself through its hiddenness*, and which conceals its greatness in the small and scarcely noticeable. After being thoroughly mocked by all and sundry, chasteness and moderation are visibly on the wane in various areas of life, including religion. I do not think that God has abandoned them though.

. 6 .

The Tribulations of a Believing Scientist

I have a friend who is a physicist, a Catholic, and a nice man, who occasionally attends meetings of the clergy and gives them talks about developments in contemporary physics. He is motivated by the three aforementioned aspects of his character, and his efforts always evoke my praise and admiration. I personally am kindly excused from ever attending clergy meetings because of the demands of my university teaching. Nevertheless I voluntarily make the effort to attend "at least once a year," preferably during Lent or Advent. ("Am I to choose you a penance or would you like to suggest one yourself?" my father confessor regularly asks me at the end of my confessions. I reflect for a moment on whether my sins have really been so onerous, and then I sigh, raise my eyes to heaven, and declare resignedly: "I shall attend the vicariate conference.")

My self-sacrificing friend recently confided in me one of his

concerns. At the end of his talks the members of the clergy in-
directly urge him as a Christian and a "believing scientist" to
leave them with at least a "tiny proof" that they might use in
their homilies to show that modern science provides proof of
the existence of God. They are nice folks and he is nice too, but
in this particular instance he cannot help them, and this wor-
ries him.

I avoid clergy meetings not because I don't like these
nice people, my brother priests, or because I feel in any way
superior—I have no reason to—but for just one simple reason:
almost every time I attend I am painfully assailed by a mixture
of sadness, pity, and hopelessness, a sense that in spite of the
self-sacrifice and goodwill of many priests, this world is "jinxed."
I can't rid myself of the feeling that somewhere deep in their
hearts, most of these nice old gentlemen are aware of something
that it took me a long time to admit, namely, that a certain mode
of religion (the post-Enlightenment religion of the past two centuries, whose theology they studied and to whose service they
have devoted so much effort) is on its way out, and there is no
stopping it. It's no longer difficult to envisage the time when "not
a stone of it will be left on another."

I find the subject matter of such meetings so surprising
that on occasions I have timidly broached the questions "What
do you think will become of all this? What will be left of this
Church in fifty years' time?" But the responses I receive leave
me feeling as if I am in the family of a chronically ill person,
where there is a tacit agreement that the illness must never
be mentioned. And if I may be permitted to say something
really dreadful: I have subsequently even had the feeling, in
certain church surroundings, that I have been catapulted into
Sartre's play *No Exit*, the one, where, after a while, the audience realizes that all the protagonists are dead but behave as if

nothing has happened.[1] One Czech priest once compared our Church to a mill that still clattered away but no longer ground anything.

Things have improved since then, of course, and I have at last found my place among the Czech clergy (sufficiently at the edge so that I can continue to "see out," and sufficiently inside not to be a total "outsider"). In most cases we are simply more used to each other by now; I have a few more friends among them than I used to have a few years ago, but there is still a lack of mutual understanding between myself and many of the clergy, and I don't expect that to change—I am no longer capable of speaking their language and they cannot understand mine. I am afraid our experiences of life, our emotional worlds, and our style of thinking are too remote from each other by now.

I advise my physicist friend to speak plainly. Science can never prove the existence of God. *"A scientifically proven god" would not be worthy of our belie*f—it would be an idol. *"Si comprehendis, non est Deus,"* said Saint Augustine, and it is necessary to take that deadly seriously: if you can grasp (and even "prove" it!), then you can be absolutely sure that it is *not* God.

The priests' pleading for a tiny little proof indicates not simply a possibly excusable incompetence in the matter of contemporary science and philosophy, but also, more depressingly, a rather less excusable *theological* incompetence, and in particular, a weak, sickly faith. A complex-ridden form of faith that is also so unwilling and unable to open itself to Mystery that it demands that science should provide a patch for its uncertainties is too flawed and rotten to be worth patching. It is "salt that has lost its savor" and is fit only to be thrown away and trodden underfoot (which happens, anyway, all over the place). Literature such as *The Bible as History*, which seeks to use the supreme authority of the Enlightenment—"science as the only arbiter of truth"—to mollify and reassure a religion shaken by the Enlightenment, indicates a cowardly and insanely suicidal form of religion.[2]

Nor, of course, can science "disprove God." A scientist who declares that he has used scientific means to refute religion is a charlatan who has ceased to practice science and become an amateur theologian. He has exceeded his competence and abused the authority of science to support his belief, his religion—that is, atheism, and it is just as dishonorable as what insecure believers would like to manipulate a "believing scientist" into doing.

Religion, faith, and theology have no right to interfere in the internal concerns of science, or meddle in physics and biology. If they fail to stand aside and respect the absolute freedom and independence of science qua science, any "pious" intervention will fare just as badly and lead to a similar discrediting of religion as happened in the past, when such interference was supported by political interests and the power of the state.

Likewise, science must maintain a consistently detached attitude to faith and religion, and particularly avoid any attempts to prove or refute "the existence of God"; otherwise it will compromise itself and betray its integrity. A scientist "disproving God" is just as pathetic as Gagarin's alleged report to the Central Committee of the Communist Party of the Soviet Union that he had seen no God through the window of his spaceship (much to the relief, no doubt, of the Soviet high priests of atheism). And we should add that a scientist "proving God" is no less pathetic.

Naturally one can be *captivated* by the beauty, symmetry, and purposefulness of nature, even in the midst of scientific activity. But a "god of reason" that might emerge from such an enchantment would equally bear little resemblance to the God of my faith. Instead, I would suspect the assertion of such a concept would be "wishful thinking," and I regard it as a mirror of our own *enchantment with our own reason*, which we project onto nature when we "discover the laws of nature."

The shift in physical and philosophical concepts from the idea of a "purposeful universe" to "chaos theory" (or so-called chaotic events in nonlinear dynamic systems) is much more in tune with my faith, because it seems to me to be an *analogy* with the main characteristic of God that we can "discern," namely, *His inconceivability*. Of course, in this case also, this is more a matter of *my own* meditation on the meditations of scientists, rather than "tracking down" the fact that this is *really* happening.

Does this mean that "science" and "religion" are two utterly separate spheres, which neither can nor should have any mutual encounter, and that any attempts at "dialogue" and cooperation are pointless? By no means! Such a dialogue is extremely important for both sides, particularly nowadays, and especially for our shared world. But the sphere in which this dialogue can and must take place, and whose rules it must respect, is *philosophy*.

The point is that science and religion, or more accurately, scientists and people of faith, particularly theologians, almost never remain confined within their own disciplines, and invariably venture into the territory of philosophy.

There is nothing wrong with that per se. It is not only natural; it is clearly unavoidable. What is simply required is that both sides should be aware of and acknowledge it—and above all, that neither side should indulge in cheap-jack or dilettante philosophy.

Frequently, alas, this is not what happens—on both sides. Many declarations by scientists, posing as *scientific* standpoints and claiming the authority of science, have very little to do with science qua science, but are a *philosophical* position, which tends to be some *philosophical reflection on scientific knowledge*, sometimes interesting, original, and perceptive, and at other times dubitable. (Even an outstanding scientific specialist can sometimes turn out to be a dilettante when it comes to philosophy.)

Similarly, one can sometimes encounter "statements of faith" by theologians and Church authorities, claiming the authority of the Church, Scripture, and even God Himself, which are in reality *philosophical reflections* about faith, religious symbols, "faith experiences," or scriptural testimonies—sometimes profound, sometimes problematical, but always *human* and always contingent on history and culture.

If scientists want to look up from their microscopes and theologians from the folios of Scripture and say something to the world about them, they have no choice but to borrow the language and techniques of philosophy. After all, they already operate within the ambit of many philosophical traditions and "pre-understandings." Even when strictly positivist scientists and fundamentalist believers (these very similar twins who cannot abide each other because of their unacknowledged similarity, and whose mutual skirmishes create the impression that science and faith must live in enmity) vituperate against philosophy as vacuous speculation and meddlesome dilution of their sole truths and certainties, they are adopting philosophical positions, albeit somewhat primitive ones. The rejection of philosophy is a philosophical stance, just as systematic apoliticism is a political standpoint and militant atheism is a kind of religion. In all cases, a peevish and undifferentiating *anti* is a sign of an attitude that could do with some philosophical self-reflection if it is to move from the shallows into the depths.

The desire to do without the lengthy and strenuous work of philosophical reflection and derive a would-be "philosophy" or "world outlook" directly from scientific knowledge has dismal results similar to when certain preachers, waving the Bible in one hand and a hamburger in the other, harangue us at stadiums or from our television screens with information about what God's current intentions are for us.

The "scientific worldview" or "scientific atheism" was one of the most debased forms of *religion* in history. It was *scientists*, rather than the apologists of belief, who should have been honor-bound to protest against such besmirching and abuse of the reputation and authority of science.

The first job of a genuine philosophy of science should be to sweep away for good all the surviving remnants of experiments in "scientific philosophy" and also the latent projection of a dilettante philosophy (or, more accurately, an ideology, such as the materialism of the later Enlightenment and the theories of its successors) into the sphere of science and the interpretation of scientific discoveries. Nowadays, when one converses with certain respected scientists—genuine specialists in their fields—not only about "purely philosophical" matters, but also about various practical issues related to the application of some of the achievements of science and technology in our civilization and their consequences for human life, as well as about burning issues of scientific ethics, it is sometimes astonishing to discover the latent philosophies that still underlie their responses. Echoes of former training in Marxism-Leninism or shallow scientism are sometimes securely lodged in the "subcortex" of otherwise extremely efficient brains inside the heads of those who would never willingly admit anything of the kind. Only scientists who do not behave in the field of philosophy like bulls in a china shop can be truly useful partners in a "dialogue between science and religion."

But this applies just as much to the other side. It would definitely never occur to anyone to invite a primitive religious fundamentalist or militant apologist to dialogue with scientists, unless the intention was not to have a genuine debate but simply an entertaining TV show. A theologically *educated* and theologically *thinking* person (unfortunately the one does not necessarily guarantee the other) is more likely to be called upon.

By its nature, theology is infinitely closer to philosophy than is science. Although they both emerged in a specific philosophical context and climate, theology can be said to have had an easier task: the Platonism and Aristotelianism that molded the first centuries of theological development, as well as the hermeneutic philosophy that largely influences theology nowadays, are infinitely more productive and profounder than the enlightened rationalism and subsequent materialism and positivism that exercised a fatal influence on the evolution of modern science.

It must be said that in the post-Enlightenment period, theology was also ensnared by attempts to create a "fixed system," one that would make as good an impression on people looking for certainties as "scientific truth"—that self-confident bastion of modern rationalism. Admittedly, that neo-scholastic system is generally regarded these days in theological circles as being just as inapplicable as is the mechanistic model of the universe of Newtonian physics in scientific circles. Neither in science, nor in theology—and not at all in philosophy—can one yearn for "fixed systems" of secure knowledge. What now prevails is a constant *movement of thought*, which, if it were to say to any particular moment of its development, "Stay awhile, you are so lovely," it would sink into hell along with Doctor Faust.

There are also many top-class *specialists* among theologians, working in a whole range of different disciplines, such as the exegesis of biblical texts or ecclesiastical history. However, although they can enrich the discussion with scientists in interesting ways, the main partner in such a debate should be *philosophical theology*. (The term "philosophy of religion" is too burdened with the "philosophy of genitives" of the Enlightenment, while the term "natural theology" is encumbered by confusion in modern times surrounding the concept of "nature"; although "fundamental theology" is a term commonly used in Catholic theological circles for what I have in mind, outside that context it is likely to evoke unfortunate associations because of the word "fundamentalism"—albeit the purpose of "fundamental theology" is precisely to dispel the danger of fundamentalism, and transfer thinking into that area of pre-understanding of faith, where, if *thinking* is absent, the dangerous virus of fundamentalist "certainties" becomes rife.)

Allow me to introduce into this debate several ideas from the writing of a leading representative of contemporary Catholic philosophical theology, Nicholas Lash, a professor at Cambridge University. I am convinced that his thinking in particular can help in a fundamental way to eliminate several crucial confusions that have long had a baneful influence on the relationship between science and Christian faith.[3]

Lash shows how the perception of the concept of God underwent a major shift in European—and particularly British—culture at the time of the Enlightenment. That was when people first started to use the concept of God to explain the *causes* of the physical universe.

Professor Lash explains that the earlier Scholastic concept of *causa* was much more comprehensive and differentiated. It did far more than simply denote a physical cause; the concept also embraced meaning and purpose—*why* a specific object is here. In the seventeenth and eighteenth centuries, thinkers felt a need to find and name one specific principle from which they could deduce the origin and operation of the world's machinery—and the religious concept of "God" suited their purpose fairly well. Later, science entered a phase in which it discovered that it no longer needed one simple ultimate explanatory principle, because nothing of the kind was sufficient to explain the complex reality of the world—so naturally, that concept was discarded. However, that methodological issue related to the world of physics gave rise to the wrongful philosophical and theological deduction that "God doesn't exist."[4]

But the God that Christian faith talks about doesn't belong to the world of physics at all. God is not a "physical cause of the world," but the *mystery of its meaning.*

Nicholas Lash draws attention to another major confusion—with respect to the term *creation.* When physicists (and theologically uninformed Christians also, unfortunately) talk about creation they are again thinking in terms of *an event of a physical order*: the moment and course of "the beginning of the universe."

When theology talks about creation, it is referring to something else—creation as *the whole of reality,* everything that *is not God*: people, animals, the material universe, works of music, and everything else we can think of. *We are creation.* What is important for faith and theology is that we are creation, that is, that we were created; how and when and what was the "physical cause" of the universe—those are questions for physics that have nothing to do with faith or theology.

When people on either side laboriously compare the various changing hypotheses about the origins of the universe (the "Big Bang" theory, etc.) with biblical texts, particularly the first chapter of Genesis, in order to prove how much they tally or not, and "prove" or "disprove" so-called biblical truth by means of physics, it is, in all events, a senseless exercise.

In my view, such analyses give rise to a number of very important conclusions for "the science and faith dialogue," which I have once more become aware of in recent weeks. In essence, what theology tells us by its teaching about creation is that *we are not God,* but that whether or not we realize it, we are all—believers, atheists, mosquitoes, and the planet Saturn—*in a relationship to the mystery* that we call God. This teaching is of enormous importance because it binds us morally to a specific stance of respect, humility, and responsibility; however, it is absolutely unimportant and irrelevant for those seeking answers about when and how the universe came into existence, or about biological aspects of evolution, and so forth.

Quite often people inform me with a friendly nod and a wink that "they are believers too." They are not "church attenders as such," but they are convinced (or rather they have the feeling, because, after all there isn't time to *ponder* such things) that "it couldn't all have come into existence by chance, could it?"—"There has to be *something*." For that reason they also consider themselves Christians, because perhaps they have a vague inkling that Christians believe in the creation and the Creator (and anyway, all religions are about the same thing aren't they, Father Halík, when all is said and done?!).

I must admit I seldom have the courage to resolutely disabuse them of that nonsensical mishmash and tell them straight out that their views about the origin of the world and the choice between the Big Bang and "the watchmaker who must have wound the thing up in the first place," as well as attempts to reconcile such interpretations and declare them to be the same, have as little to do with Christian faith as their choice between jazz and Bach, or between beer and wine.

Christian faith has absolutely nothing to do with speculation about the physical causes of the world's origins. When Christians confess their faith in the words "I believe in God . . . creator of heaven and earth," they are not saying that they think that "it was all done in the beginning by some great big invisible uncle behind the scenes"—such speculation is entirely their "private affair" and is totally irrelevant from the point of view of faith—but are thereby *committing themselves to an attitude of respect toward the world.* They are affirming that the world is a *gift entrusted to them.*

Faith is not a compendium of opinions about the nature of the donor—all we know about Him is that He is absolute mystery, incomprehensible per se, yet revealed nonetheless in His *actions*—in the fact that the world exists, that Jesus was with us as a man and He remains as His Word to us; in the fact that there exists a community of believers, maintained and renewed, in spite of all its weaknesses, by His Spirit. Accepting each of these realities (the world, Jesus, the Church), not as mere chance facts but as *His gift*, whereby He communicates with us and introduces Himself, and *responding* to it with one's life, one's prayers of praise, and one's attitude to those realities—that is faith, that is Christian existence.[5]

I make so bold as to assert that the absolute majority of the two billion Christians living *today* on this planet are fully aware that literary depictions of the "act of creation," whether it be the text in the book of Genesis, Michelangelo's frescoes on the ceiling of the Sistine Chapel, or Jean Effel's charming cartoon film *The Creation of the World*, are symbolic images that are not to be taken "literally" or regarded as reportage about "how it really was," but are instead an illustration of a certain truth that is "beyond" those images directed at our imagination. (Perhaps the Czech Republic was the only place in 2005 where a university teacher would ask you if it was all right for her to receive Communion if, although she was baptized, she believed in Darwin's Origin of the Species. Naturally I told her that it *wasn't*, but not on account of her belief in Darwin's theory, but because she needed to supplement her knowledge of what Christians do and do not believe to at least the standard of the catechism for primary school pupils. She could believe what she liked when it came to theories of biology or physics; that was purely a matter for her academic conscience; all her religious conscience demanded of her was to maintain an attitude of healthy criticism toward all scientific theories and not regard them *religiously* as "revealed truth.")

My fear is, however, that beneath *that truth*—described by the Bible in images borrowed from the mythology of its surroundings and by Michelangelo and Jean Effel in images from the realm of their imagination—many Christians project the non-Christian, deist concept of "the Great Watchmaker" that emerged in modern times. It will require a great step into the depths of that mystery to clear away such notions as those. As the mystics and the best traditions of Catholic theology have taught us over centuries, "images," and not only the primitive kind but also the abstract, conceptual products of our speculations, must eventually be left behind: faith consists in the orientation of our existence, in our basic attitudes in this life, not in what we foster at the superficial level of our minds, where our notions and our "opinions about this or that" reside. If there is something about which you have "a firm opinion"—to paraphrase Saint Augustine once more—then you can be sure that it is not God.

At the end of your life God's assessment of how you have responded *in faith* to the truth about creation revealed by God is more likely to be done by weighing up how you actually *behaved* toward the world around you rather than by considering what you *thought* about the world and how it came into existence. What the epistle of James says about faith being capable of demonstration solely by works[6] fully applies in this case. It is a much more profound assertion than the fairly trivial statement that people should also behave in accordance with their faith—faith is that which is *implicit* in what you do and the attitudes you adopt!

But to return to the previous considerations: How do I conceive a "dialogue between science and faith," how should it proceed, and what should be its purpose?

If physicists talk about how the universe arose and biologists about how the evolution of animal species occurred, theologians will have to place their hands over their mouths and listen in silence, because their particular domain has nothing to say about these matters. But the moment that a physicist starts to talk about how his discoveries have great potential for improving the next type of weapon of mass destruction, or a biologist states that it is not only technically possible but also morally justified to clone human individuals and manufacture embryos for use in experiments, and so on, then the theologians will be obliged to stand up and tell their colleagues from the world of science in no uncertain terms that they have gone beyond the bounds of their competency and entered territory where theology also has something to say.

At that moment the theologians are bound to speak out, because they know that life, and human life in particular, is not *only* a biophysical event, but also a gift, and although we are not the givers, we have a responsibility to protect that life. This responsibility cannot be abdicated in favor of the "spontaneous development" of science and technology, market demand, or public opinion polls. Yes, at that moment a debate can commence.

Should a theologian happen to read out from Scripture, for example, the well-known passage about the creation of the earth, then he is duty-bound—because he is not a mechanical reciter, but an interpreter of texts, an exegete—to warn his listeners that he is not putting forward an alternative physical or biological theory, or "reportage about how things happened," but a text cobbled together from various different accounts, which, while borrowing the language and notions of Near Eastern mythology, gives a fundamentally different account than those mythologies:

this is not a contest between two principles of good and evil, but instead a symphony, in which one particular motif—"*it was good*"—is repeated.

It is a symphony that is unfinished. According to a venerable theological tradition running from Augustine to Karl Rahner and Nicholas Lash,[7] creation is not "manufacturing" or "making" the world, as the Enlightenment deists imagined it, but instead *creatio continua*: a continuous process. Praying, Saint Augustine said, means closing one's eyes and realizing that God is creating the world *now*. However, it is also a symphony that clearly implies a gradation toward a finale. Appreciation of this gradation is called "the virtue of faith," and the finale indicated is called "*shalom*," the great peace that will come about when *God will be all in all*.

And if a theologian will say this, then it will be the turn of the physicist and biologist to put their hands over their mouths, because their researches make no mention of anything of the kind. *As scientists*, there is nothing they can add to it, neither to confirm nor to refute it. But because scientists are not just scientists but are also people who philosophize, who listen to music and the murmur of the forest, who have their beliefs and their doubts, their anxieties and their hopes, this will not, of course, be a "dialogue of the deaf" (as we might describe "the history of disputes between science and belief"), but the opportunity for an enriching human encounter.

"My dear Jan," I tell my physicist friend, "next time you go to a clergy meeting and I receive an invitation to a learned society or one of the institutes of the Academy of Sciences, and we are both confronted in the main by tired old gentlemen who have been conditioned by what the centuries of misunderstanding between the two worlds have accumulated, let us not fall prey to skepticism. This epoch calls for people who are able to build bridges and do what they can to see that prejudice and suspicion give way to the courage to trust."

And so, even though I don't think I have been particularly sinful since my last confession, I am resolving to make an effort to attend one clergy meeting before this book comes out at Christmas.

The Joy of Not Being God

"Religion is a crutch for the weak. I don't need a god—I'm my own god," a young man declared resolutely during a public debate I attended.

I don't know about you, I thought to myself, but I really couldn't recommend myself for the role of God. But I have no wish to ridicule him or cause him offense, so I simply asked with a slight touch of irony: "But don't you find it boring? I'm afraid by now I'm fairly well aware of what I can expect of myself, whereas my God never ceases to surprise me. I prefer to spend my time in places that have a *wide open vista* rather than a closed window."

I would also have liked to add that one of the greatest joys of my faith, of my reliance on God, is precisely the assurance that I am "permanently exempt from playing God." It is possibly an even greater joy than the longed for verdict that I was "excused from P.E." would have been during my school years, or that I was "exempt from military service" during the years of the Warsaw Pact. Neither of those hopes were realized, however. I think of the Jesuit Anthony de Mello's joyful exclamation that he had finally renounced the role of director of the universe!

But I didn't say it. It seemed to me that the young man's "divinity" would have to come up against a bit more life experience before he grew tired of it and it ceased to be a temptation.

How many times have I heard such views already? Perhaps Nietzsche put it most aptly: if God existed how could I bear not being God? Throughout modern times this dilemma of "*either* I *or* He" has occurred to many people, not just philosophers, in relation to Nietzsche's concept of humanity and godhead. And if it was posed in those terms, the answer was obvious: I, of course! So long as that same dilemma culminated in the choice of "religion *or* freedom" it is not entirely surprising that people rejected religion.

But then one wise old Jew, who resembled the biblical prophets not only on account of his patriarchal appearance, stepped forward and presented the problem differently: either I and it, or I and *Thou*.

Either the dominant human "I" will be at the center, taught Martin Buber, and such an "I" will have a *subject-object* relationship with the world, other people, and—should it recognize God—to God also; its world will be the "realm of the world of *it*." "It" can be anything that people think they can manipulate as needed, or at least that they can treat—and speak about—with a certain detachment, as if it were something *external*.

The only alternative is the sort of *I* that fundamentally needs and demands a partner, "a sort of primordial Thou." Indeed, only by its relationship with Thou is such an "I" and its entire world established. For people "Thou" is what they cannot manipulate; it is not "under their control"; it is what they must respect and allow to come to them in all its difference. For Buber the "absolute Thou" is God and only God. God is the *horizon* creating the space in which everything can change for us from "It" into "Thou"—not just other people, but also the landscape, a flower, a tree, or a book. It can speak to me *unconditionally*.

Buber resolutely rejected Sartre's comment that every "Other" can be that "Thou" and something like that has no need for God: according to Buber, I cannot be permanently and exclusively in an "I and Thou" relationship with any Other; in certain situations every *Other* becomes an *It* for me, so I can and sometimes must keep my distance from It. What I cannot keep my distance from, however, is God: the moment I start to talk about God "in the third person," objectively—to regard or treat Him as some object within this world—God is transformed into an idol for me.

Analogically to Saint Augustine's dictum, already quoted several times in this book: "*Si comprehendis, non est Deus,*"[1] Buber maintains that *what you relate to as an "object"* is not and cannot be God. God can be experienced solely in a personal relationship; the prototype of such a relationship is prayer.

God is not "something near" (first, because He is not a "thing"; and second, because He is infinitely distant in His incomprehensibility, unfathomability, and unobjectifiableness), but rather God is *nearness* itself. God is light, declared Saint Bonaventure, repeating the well-known expression in Scripture, and he went on to say that when we look we do not see the "light" itself, but we see all things *in the light*. Rather than seeking God in the world, we can *contemplate the world in God,* in the divine light, without mistaking the world for God, or God for the world in the process.

Inadvertently, the young fellow who said he was his own god was right in one way, I thought to myself at the end of that public debate. *At the outset* the human individual "finds itself in the position of God"—it is not until the moment of conversion, real change of heart (*metanoia*), which is the origin and foundation of a living faith, that our *I* is "suspended" from that position. And of course there are people who have never experienced that conversion and have never opened their self-centered world to an absolute Thou, and who remain forever, often unthinkingly and unaware, in that "godlike position." They can be people who regard themselves as atheists, but equally they can be people who live in some sort of religious belief that has not undergone this restructuring of their world, "conversion," an existential conversion from the world of I-It to the world of I-Thou. To the great detriment of themselves and their nearest, I would add.

Unlike religion, which is inherited and is linked to tradition and authority, faith is something that comes into existence through *conversion*: sometimes conversion from atheism, or these days more likely from an unthinking "godlessness"— ignorance of those matters that formerly people "automatically" (willy-nilly, uncritically, unquestioningly) absorbed from the surroundings in which they grew up. On other occasions it is conversion from some kind of "neo-pagan religiosity," which abounds everywhere, or the abandonment of the traditional, inherited ("popular" or even "folkloric") Christian religiosity of their childhood. Such conversions tend not to be instant events; they are mostly lengthy processes that consist of repeated periods of doldrums, crisis, and revival. This is because faith is not a "worldview"; it is not merely espousing a specific "persuasion" and certainly not something static or fixed. Real living faith is a permanent battle with our "I," which was shifted from the "position of god" at the moment of our conversion, but nevertheless constantly endeavors to regain that position. What theology terms *sin* is not simply "error" or "breaking the rules of the moral code," but above all an act whereby our "I" once more strives for a while to regain its lost position. It is an act directed against the living God, the "absolute Thou," whom we invited through our conversion into the center and focal point of our lives, and now we are once more denying Him that status.

The point is that God's dwelling in man is paradoxical. It encompasses *already* and *not yet*: this mystery "already" *dwells* within us, while at the same time it is always *yet to come*. Hope and faith are the forces that defend the freedom and openness of our souls for this mystery, for God. If faith and hope do not live in us, then "God's" place is readily taken by something else. The most importunate pretender to that throne is usually our self-centered *I*. The problem is that whatever usurps God's place doesn't become God, thereby, but an idol. "Their eyes were opened and they saw they were naked," says the Bible in the description of the prototype of this situation: the vain attempt to seize God's place and His privileges.

What do I mean when I say that the human "I" is already in the *position of god* "at the outset," and what is the origin of this situation? I am referring to that *self-centeredness*, the state in which our *I* is not subject to the corrective or refining influence of a *Thou* that matters more to the "I" than the "I" does to itself. If my self-centeredness wins out, then I truly am "my own god" (whatever my "views about God" might be).

There are two ways of explaining the fact that the human "I" is "at the outset" already in this position, before we are even aware of it and before we can do anything about it through our own free will. They are very different, because each of them belongs to a different intellectual discipline. One is theological, the other psychological. And yet I don't feel that they are conflicting or mutually exclusive, or that we must necessarily choose one *or* the other, particularly when we realize that neither is an "explanation of the cause" of this phenomenon, so much as a way of understanding (interpreting) its sense. Maybe we will bear both in mind, as different keys to opening the same room with many doors; maybe we will tend to use the one that is closer to our style of thinking and vocabulary.

One of these explanations is much older, older than Christianity itself, and has a bearing on the biblical narrative about the fall of the first man. The other is fairly modern; it is the theory of primordial narcissism, advanced by the more recent "revisionist" younger wave of psychoanalysis, particularly in the Anglo-Saxon world.

The Genesis narrative about the sin of the first human couple entered the Christian subconscious chiefly thanks to Saint Paul's—and subsequently, above all, Saint Augustine's—interpretation of it as "original sin." I consider this doctrine one of Christianity's most realistic and valuable contributions to the philosophy of anthropology, the study of human beings and their nature. Nevertheless, in our day it is not easy to get to the heart of that doctrine; we come up against the mythological literary form of the biblical message, and an alien—and, moreover, truly confusing—terminology, as well as certain problematical features of Augustine's theology.

The terminological pitfalls were highlighted by Karl Rahner, the greatest Catholic theologian of the twentieth century, when he opened his exposition of the dogma of "original sin" by saying that it was first necessary to realize that it was neither "original"—that is, something unique to be transmitted—nor a "sin" in the way that the term is generally understood. The "original sin" is not something "inherited" in a biological or genetic sense; the word "sin" in this case does not indicate some single "immoral act," but a *state* in which human existence finds itself.

The dynamic description of the polarity of human existence between the Old Adam, in whom all sinned, and the New Adam—Christ—through whom all are saved, as we read in Paul's letter,[2] collides with today's personalistic and individualistic understanding of man. We find it hard to think in terms of Paul's categories of the "collective person," his perception of Adam and Christ as "types of humankind," rather than two individual humans.

Saint Augustine formulated his doctrine of original sin in his dispute with Pelagius and his understanding of Christian existence as a moral *act*; in doing so he defended something of enormous worth, namely, the precedence of God's love and mercy (*a gift*) over human merit. However, when reading the many texts in which Augustine designates the essence of "original sin" with the word *concupiscentia* "lust," the psychologically schooled reader is almost bound to sense shadows of the saint's personal problems creeping in—namely his distinctive, raw, and obsessively neurotic attitude to sexuality and his own erotic past. (Augustine, who wrote all too much about such matters and also much about himself, naturally risked the eventuality that his readers, even many centuries later, would think—rightly or wrongly—that they "could read his mind," to a greater degree than he would probably have found pleasant; lo, a mild warning for anyone tempted to follow in his footsteps!)

As I have already mentioned, modern psychology approaches the matter of the origins of self-centeredness from a slightly different angle. A small child regards itself quite naturally as the center of the universe, and the people and objects around it as something it can move around like its big toe. It is accustomed to the world being as close as its mother's breast, ready at every instant to satisfy its wants. However, until the child grows into the world of relationships and discovers *Thou* as something that must be respected as something radically different, it does not discover its own "*I.*" It is characteristic that during the first years after a child first learns to speak, it talks about itself also in the third person. The "grandiose self" and "narcissism" of the small child is actually rooted in an enormous indiscriminate "things happen," out of which subsequently emerges a conscious subject "*I*"—together with the ability to respect *Thou*. Some psychoanalysts regard this primary narcissism not only as a prototype or analogy of possible subsequent personality disorders, but the actual germ thereof, in view of its preoccupation with self and an inability to be truly open to the world and experience fully fledged and responsible relationships.

The British school of "object-relations theory" focuses on the role of *objects* that can attract the child's attention and assist it in the process of freeing itself from itself and realistically integrating itself into the surrounding world. These objects can be things, particularly toys, or fairy tales, or fantastic/religious images, or beings that abound in the child's world and broaden the sphere *between* "inside" and "outside." In general, "God" also first becomes part of the child's awareness in the company of entire armies of such images, but whereas fairies and elves eventually disappear beyond recall, "God" can remain—but our concept of Him changes throughout our lives, as we absorb not only what we hear and read about Him but also our own personal, and not simply "religious," life experience.

Interestingly this concerns not only "believers" but also atheists. Karl Rahner once splendidly stated that "God's story relates to everyone, believer and atheist alike"; one could invert this and say that everyone's story, whether they are believers or atheists, relates to God. Like believers, atheists also have some notion about God, except that they assign Him a different ontological status. And we should add that people's notions about God are extremely varied, and the border between them by no means constitutes a demarcation line between believers and nonbelievers: a pathologically punitive celestial policeman is for some an object of derision and antipathy, while for others he is a terrorizing, omnipresent God, whom they look up to at every moment; a kind and merciful God is for some an object of reverence and the recipient of their prayers, while for others He is a childish illusion and the opium of the people.

"The question is not whether God exists," a Czech logician and mathematician recently wrote in response to some questionnaire or other, "—of course God exists—at the very least as a word in our vocabulary. The problem is what sort of existence we assign Him." God can exist for someone as a notion that is unconnected with any experience, but God is rarely void of images, feelings, or associations. People can suppose that "God exists" as a human idea, or that He exists like a chair or a cuckoo, or alternatively like a "supernatural being" behind the scenes of the visible world, or as "energy," or "truth," or a "number." People can assign their "yes, I believe," or "I deny," or "I don't know" to any of these notions of the existence of God. They can imagine that "God exists objectively" or "only subjectively"—at least until they encounter someone versed in theology who will inform them that *neither* of those answers is appropriate: if we want to think about God theologically we must first demolish the stage set erected in modern times: the fictive division of the world into "objective" and "subjective." I will recall on several occasions in this book Thomas Aquinas's absolutely fundamental dictum that the outcome of his theological analyses is the conviction that *we do not know what "being" means in the case of God*, because our experience of being is limited. It was precisely this blessed uncertainty that opened the door to the most important philosophical achievements of later centuries: the analyses of *various meanings of the verb "to be."*

Today I want to set off on a different tack: If *we do not know what God is like* or *what* God is "in essence," and yet our faith, hope, and love (as well as Scripture and doctrine and the tradition of the Church, if we are willing to accept these authorities as authorities) assure us that *God is*, that fact fundamentally changes our notion of the world and our relationship with reality.

At that moment the world ceases to be what on the surface we believe we can survey and possibly take control of; we start to reckon with a new dimension—*a mystery*, indeed, the "absolute mystery": the kind that is "bottomless."

Reality, then, is bottomless, it is *radically open*—and hence our minds and our hearts must remain *open*. We must remain attentive, alert, and respectful of the Mystery: we cannot break into it, take control of it, subdue it, or do away with it, "be done with it." All we can do is be quietly open and aware that the Mystery is not a "thing"; it is not inanimate, blind, and deaf, nor is it indifferent or dumb.

Its *language*, however, has nothing to do with spiritualist séances or some romantically mysterious "whisper in the heart" into which we could easily project our sentimentality and our wishes. *Its speech is life itself,* life that is a constant corrective (sometimes painful) to our wishes and illusions.

But God will start to speak through our lives only on one condition: *that we abandon the "throne of God" that we consciously or unwittingly occupy*—because it is so far away from our appointed place that the voice that is ordained for us and calls to us cannot reach it. So long as we play at God, or we put something in His place that we worship as a god, we cannot encounter God. When we barricade ourselves from God—by deifying ourselves or something else "that is not God" (and that is a definition of "the world" or "creation")—then we won't hear Him. If people who have absolutized or deified themselves, or any other relative value, declare "there is no God," then we must concede in their favor that this statement could be an honest and realistic reflection of their momentary experience of God's absence, their remoteness from God; it would be more accurate, however, to say that they are not aware of Him, that they "don't hear His voice."

No one hears God continuously, however; faith is life, which also consists of moments (and sometimes long stages of the journey) when we are confronted by God's silence—even he who was the Incarnation of God's Word experienced that desolation in Gethsemane and on the cross. All the more imperative, therefore, is the call of the psalmist: "If you hear His voice do not harden your hearts." We must remain *open* and leave the "highest place within us" open for Him, to whom alone it belongs.

If that fellow who claimed he was his own god was at least half serious about his godness it could be the sign of a dandy narcissistic disorder, I thought to myself.

In addition to those who believe in God and those who refute God, there are plenty who don't concern themselves about Him at all. Whether they regard themselves as atheists or "Christians" (in the sense that they were baptized and by family tradition "belong to the club"), when asked about their notion of God they reply that they have no time for such notions; when the subject of God is raised they prefer to have a beer or switch on the TV, or say anything that comes into their head—and it is patently obvious from what they say that they have never given a thought to these matters. Sometimes I can't help thinking that most of what I hear in my own country these days "in the public arena" on the subject of religion, faith, and God falls into the aforementioned category; it is quite likely that the same was true about what the young man said. He simply spoke and meant no harm by what he said, because he *wasn't thinking at all* at that moment; that is something that happens in certain talkative civilizations that regard thinking as a "luxury." "That's of interest to that intellectual one percent of yours," I was once told with due contempt by the director of a successful commercial TV channel, who knew that the universe was an aggregate of data, and he was duly proud of the fact that he had the key to it in his pocket, because he knew for certain the value of every piece of information thanks to his "people meters."

But it is precisely those people who "do not think about God" and can't even be bothered to deny Him who tend to be most defenseless against the temptation to let *anything* occupy that highest place within themselves. But if they fall prey to the temptation, they waste a great opportunity for their lives to cease being a "monologue," or their own voices to stop being drowned out by the din of the world—and instead entering into a dialogue—whereby they would be capable of *apprehending reality and life as a meaningful language* (one that frequently acts as a healthy corrective to our constant internal blather); they would be capable of listening, understanding, and responding.

When I am asked by young women believers if they can marry a "nonbeliever," the first thing I advise them is to diagnose his "unbelief," because many very diverse attitudes fall under that label. If it means that the person is "his own god," then I would advise them to be extremely cautious; home life with a god like that can be fairly tough. (Although it must be said that among those who never stop talking about God and for whom church is "home away from home" there are some who make room for worship of a "domestic idol.") Faith, if it is a living faith, provides permanent prevention against and therapy for the disease of *self-deification*—that disease whose perniciousness is often overlooked for the sole reason that we live in a culture that is not only permeated with the disease but often proclaims it as a virtue: the summit and fulfillment of human life—as "self-fulfillment."[3]

One of the fundamental features of faith is *trust*. The neurotic urge to play God and have everything under one's control is often the result of a fearfully distrustful attitude to life, a feeling that the unknown always conceals a potential danger. "Students, whenever I can't get to sleep, I think about how to get the whole universe into a state of combat readiness," we used to be told by the notorious head of the reserve officers training section at the Arts Faculty before he finally went mad. I would happily give him an A+ if not for "scientific" then certainly for *existential atheism*.

Equally, the current vogue phrase that "we now have global responsibility"—unless it is simply a poetical metaphor for the essentially banal truth that "no man is an island" and "everything is interconnected"—can be the expression of that "earthly gods" arrogance that draws us into the nebulous realm of "cosmic feelings," where it is easy to forget about the actual responsibility that each of us has—not for the globe, but for what has been truly entrusted to our custody and care, and to us alone.

When we have the courage to loose from our grip the reins that don't control anything anyway, but which nonetheless drag us along all the time—through our anxieties and arrogance, through our ludicrous, yet dangerous grandiosity, foolishness, and vanity—when we give up our fictitious post of commander of the universe, we feel enormous relief. Humility and truth liberate and heal.

We spend our lives learning to listen and differentiate—and we also spend our lives learning to *let go*. Our entire life, if we start to understand its language, frees us from our notions, endeavors, ambitions, fantasies, and plans, from all the "alternative scenarios" that we might just have managed to implement, if God's kindly hand had not intervened sooner or later.

It gives me great pleasure to see a good politician, diplomat, bishop, actor, lawyer, psychotherapist, journalist, or father of a large family; one reason is that if someone is doing all these things and doing them well I get the reassuring and liberating confirmation that *I myself don't have to become those things anymore*. It helps prevent me from "looking back," and frees me from thoughts and fantasies that I might have been able to be some of those things too, and maybe I wouldn't have been bad at them. I am learning to *joyfully* let go of things and to realize that "one can't be everything"; God alone is a being that totally fulfills all His potentialities. God narrows my path and thereby He allows me to understand (perhaps) more precisely what He truly wants of me, what I cannot delegate to anyone else: simply to be Tomáš Halík. Because if I were to fail in this, then it would be the only place that would then truly remain empty. "God will not judge you for not having been Abraham, Moses, or Samson," the Hassidic Rabbi Mayer used to say—and permit me to repeat it. "God will judge whether, and to what extent, you were Mayer."

But God would judge and condemn me if I wanted to be God and if I played at God, usurped his prerogatives, and tried to ape Him; for *the ruler of this world*—the one who apes God—has been condemned.[4]

If I am utterly convinced, with the full weight of my faith, that God is—and He performs His task well—what a relief that I don't have to stand in for Him in an amateurish fashion, that I don't have to be God!

It is late evening once more and shortly I shall lie down for my "divine service of sleep"—as I have called this time ever since I meditated my way through Rahner's *theology of everyday things*. Not only "prayer before sleeping," but also sleep itself is an act of trust in God's world order, a small daily nod of the head in assent, training for the moment when we will all have to dismiss everything from our heads and our hands and control nothing at all anymore; when we will plunge ourselves totally into the mystery and surprise, of which the world of dreams—in which the impossible becomes possible—is a foretaste. May that last dream—from which we shall be awakened into the undying light of the Easter morning—be free of the anxiety and confusion that abounds in so many dreams of our nights on earth.

It is a relief to be able to lie down to sleep, having previously returned my day in prayer to God's hands, having surrendered to Him those near and far, and my morrow, yes, the whole world, including the tiny portion of it that is entrusted to my responsibility. And that, too, I will be able to deliver in full to Him. What a relief, I think to myself on the verge of sleep, when I "let go of the world"; what freedom it is, what a joy—that I'm not God!

. 8 .

There and Back Again

"So here I am again," he says with a sheepish smile as he sits down opposite me in the worn big black leather armchair in one of the studies on the third floor of the Arts Faculty of Charles University. It could be the same armchair in which I sweated through my state exam in the history of philosophy opposite Professor Patočka thirty-three years earlier. He wasn't born yet, this slim young man with his short haircut, who resembles many of those I have seen here during my years of teaching. But this former student of mine, who not only attended my lectures but also occasionally my sermons at the university church, is one I remember well, although I have heard little about him in recent years. I had simply heard that some time ago he had abandoned his quickly kindled Christianity—which hadn't had time to truly catch fire—and discovered the world of oriental spiritualities. He had become so fascinated by it, in fact, that he had disappeared for years—for good, it seemed—to some Buddhist monastery, in Thailand or possibly Sri Lanka.

He sat for a long time before saying just one brief sentence, and it was not clear from it whether it was the beginning of a longer narration, or whether he had condensed his entire experience, in oriental fashion, into a single statement that was clearly intended to please me: "So first I thought that Christianity was right, then I thought Buddhism was right, and I now again think Christianity is right." His words "here I am again" now acquired quite a new meaning.

We sit in silence gazing at each other searchingly. And when it appears to me that the young re-convert doesn't want to say any more—at least not at this moment—I take the floor. "Welcome back, then." I smile—and I also smile at my own smile when I realize what idea had inspired him. And I tell him: "In fact I welcome you not only as a lost sheep from our flock, but also as someone I can congratulate on having applied a bit of Zen wisdom to his life's journey." And I remind him of the celebrated sentence in which one of the Zen masters brilliantly summed up his journey and the fruit of his enlightenment: "First I thought mountains were mountains and forests were forests, then I thought mountains weren't mountains and forests weren't forests—and now I see once more that mountains are mountains and forests are forests."

Yes, I too once underwent something of the kind, and many people who visit me, young and not so young, testify to the same. First we thought that we could live in the world by assenting to it unreservedly through our everyday behavior and accepting its games. And then we encountered a "spiritual path"—in oriental guise (how else, since we found Christianity uninteresting, "uninspiring," and maybe slightly tainted by the world that we were leaving behind on our journey of spiritual adventure?). Just as we had hoped, after the happy and tedious hours of meditation,

drop by drop or like a sudden torrent, came the liberating realization that "everything is an illusion"—my "self" separated from
the world and the spirit was an illusion; and this world was an illusion and a veil; my yearnings, aspirations, addictions, passions,
and woes were illusions; everything had to fade away in order for
us to be free. But one day, or bit by bit, something unexpectedly
dawned on us that we hadn't read about in any book on Buddhism: that the very conviction that the world, my "self," and
everything that pertains to me were all an illusion, *was itself an
illusion*. The oriental dream faded, the fairy tale came to an end,
and we were back again: mountains were mountains once more,
my self wasn't much different from my previous self, many of my
problems remained my problems, and the forests were forests
again.

There were few who wanted to talk about it and few to whom
one could talk about it. Had it been a vain attempt to move outside our culture? Had we spoiled something—or was it supposed
to happen that way? Had we lacked perseverance—was that the
reason we had missed our goals? Was it because we lacked an
experienced master that we hadn't gotten anywhere—or had at
least some of those who had returned taken the right path? Just
as the fruit of meditation cannot be discerned from the feelings one has in the course of it or immediately afterward, but
at best in the almost imperceptible changes in one's overall
behavior and attitude to the world—often entirely invisible to
oneself—so also the answer to those questions could only come
after a certain interval.

The Zen master's statement about the mountains and forests was by no means a sigh of resignation over the time wasted
and the pointless detour. Formerly he had *thought* he could see;
now, however, he *saw*; what he saw was not "totally different"
from what he had previously thought he had found, but it also
wasn't absolutely identical with what he had known—or thought

he had known—at the outset. On a similar tack is my favorite Chassidic story from Jiří Langer's book *Nine Gates*,[1] about
the poor Jew who is goaded by his dreams to set off for distant
Prague in search of a treasure, but when he gets there he discovers that the treasure had been lying back home under his own
doorstep.

One jolly monk in a Japanese Buddhist monastery—and I
was not alone in my impression that the monks in that celebrated center of Buddhism, in contrast to the other monasteries,
looked at first sight like a bunch of Good Soldier Schweiks—
assured me that people in the West were woefully wrong in regarding enlightenment as an exalted moment when the heavens
part, celestial organs thunder in the soul, and the individual is
released at last from all his problems and becomes a saint; no,
he said, it's more like realizing you've forgotten you're wearing
sunglasses and you take them off.

Another Japanese Zen master told me something similar:
Lots of people in the West believe that Buddhists "believe in
reincarnation." But the essence of reincarnation is realizing that
the myth of reincarnation is an illusion: *nothing of the kind* exists; there is simply an eternal *now*.

And then there is the well-known cycle of pictures illustrat-
ing the Buddhist spiritual path, which culminates in *the monk's
return to the marketplace*.

I know a lot of people who set out on a spiritual journey inspired by notions of Far Eastern spirituality and then returned.
All right, let's leave out the ones who really didn't go anywhere
and for whom it was just a caricature, a fashionable flirtation
with the exotic, which soon came to an end with a slight hang-
over, like an adolescent trip to nirvana with the help of a mari-
juana cigarette. I am not referring to them.

I am talking about those whose intentions and endeavors
were sincere and who did not give up after the first crisis or whiff

of boredom, when the first flush of enthusiasm had paled. I have in mind those who, in spite of everything, after a time—and the process can be shorter or longer depending on the person, but I'm not talking about a brief period—realize that they simply don't feel at home in the oriental landscape. They came back, like the student now seated opposite me.

Perhaps the student's attitude to the spiritual journey he had acquainted himself with will indicate whether he truly did get somewhere within himself. I assume he also experienced disappointment; in monasteries, whether Catholic or Buddhist (and I have made visits to both kinds on repeated occasions—not lengthy ones admittedly, but long enough to spot the phenomenon), one sooner or later encounters "the human factor," and anyone who has brought with him illusions about heaven on earth or the angelic nature of monks will be confronted by the dilemma of whether to leave in disgust or become a realist (which doesn't mean a cynic).

Those who fail to stand the test and are unable to cope with their trauma run away in terror and mostly in the stupidest direction: they run from a Catholic monastery to the gutter press, who will be all too pleased to run their experiences as a juicy story, or from the Buddhist monastery into the arms of Christian charismatics, who will exorcise the unclean demons of false deities out of them—birds of a feather, as the saying goes.

The young man opposite me had a calm and intelligent expression, however. It did not look as if his announced return to Christianity was some frantic escape or a mere U-turn. I realized that if he asked me for spiritual guidance I had a task ahead of me: namely, to encourage him to identify and preserve all the good he had encountered in recent years ("Test everything; retain what is good," the apostle Paul writes) and also *to learn to see Christianity with new eyes.*

That really does not imply any urging on my part for him to

try creating an amateur amalgam of Christianity and Buddhism, such as is available on all the esoteric literature bookstalls. But his Christianity should now be a "Christianity of a second wind," and not an attempt to step back into the same shoes he left at home years ago (that wouldn't work anyway; he'd soon discover they were too small). His "So here I am again" means a return, but it should be a return that is not mere regression back to his past. The faith he is returning to is *the same*—identical in terms of "subject matter" and "content"; after all, *Jesus Christ is the same, yesterday, today, and forever*—but it should be *different* in its style and the depth at which he will understand and live it.

The mountains are mountains, the forests are forests once more, Christ is forever, but *we* are different.

In the splendid parable in Luke's Gospel[2] the fact that the father obviously favors the returning son over his problem-free brother is not any momentary pedagogical or psychological trick to ease the embarrassment of the wanderer and his bitter re- morse, or to dispel his fear of a beating or ridicule. The father uses words of tenderness to pacify the disgruntled dutiful elder brother. In some translations he addresses him as "child," and indeed the obedient son had remained a child, whereas the one who had wandered far from home had matured *because he had returned.*

No, I am not saying this in order to incite good Catholics to bang the church door behind them and run off to Buddhist monasteries or yoga ashrams, although I expect that charge will be cast in my teeth. I'm not urging anyone to do so. The father in the parable did not drive his son out, and he was no doubt horrified to discover how far he had strayed. But such things happen: sons set off on dangerous journeys—and only some of them return.

I'm not urging anyone to leave the fold of the Church, if they are happy within it—why ever should they? There are bound to be good and contented children of the Church and I say nothing against them, above all because I don't know many of them—pastoral care of the well-behaved is not my bailiwick. I feel that my pastoral calling, in the steps of my Lord, is first and foremost to "the lost sheep of the House of Israel." Lost sheep sometimes return too. It is necessary to do a bit more to attract them than just mutely leaving the gate to the sheepfold open.

Sometimes I make a mental apology to those I might have unjustly offended when I used to speak, often ironically, about "our homegrown Buddhists." I am aware that there is a constantly developing path of "Western Buddhism," which has many different branches and, in common with Indian Christianity, for instance, has preserved the core of the doctrine and creatively "recontextualized" it for a different environment. I realize that apart from those in the West who only flirt with oriental spiritualities, there are quite a number of people in America, Western Europe, and in our country who conscientiously, diligently, and faithfully follow in the steps of the Buddha, and this undoubtedly bears good fruit for them and those around them. I would not like to create the impression by what I have said here that I believe that sooner or later these Westerners will or ought to end up in Christianity and the Church. I respect the choice of their hearts and consciences. Naturally, as a Christian, my wish for them is that *eventually* they should end up in the embrace of Christ—but I can well imagine (and in line with absolutely orthodox Catholic doctrine I am also allowed to hope[3]) that those who continue along the path of other religions for the rest of their lives, in obedience to the voice of their conscience, will end up in that embrace for eternity.

Moreover Buddhists—including most Western Buddhists—do not regard their spiritual path or their practice as "religion," and by no means do they consider it to be "in competition" with Christianity (and let us leave aside for now the debate about the sense in which contemporary Christianity can be regarded as a "religion"). My occasional ironical comments about people who try to combine various spiritual paths also does not apply wholesale: apart from the pathetically shallow syncretism that is so widespread nowadays, there exists a phenomenon known as "multiple religious identity," which is the subject of careful examination by present-day religious scholars. A world in which different cultures will increasingly intermingle is bound to confront us with various surprises. As Christians, and particularly as theologians, we should first study these phenomena carefully, soberly, and without bias, before we come to an independent judgment. There are more than enough instances of hasty demonization in our past and we all know what they led to. Yes, the fact that many people in the West start to search spiritually outside Christianity is partly due to the fact that Christians compromised and discredited their faith in the course of history through their narrow-mindedness and their faithless premature anticipation of the Last Judgment.

But I recall the words I heard on several occasions from the lips of the Tibetan Dalai Lama: he would emphatically remind his Western listeners that he had not come to propagate Buddhism but to urge them to live to the best of their ability within their own ("home") religion. Even though, as I stress yet again, I respect those people in the West who have found a home in Buddhism, in this essay I am talking about the others of whom there are also a considerable number, those for whom their encounter with oriental spiritualities was only one chapter in their journey, and who have come to the view that they ought to return to Christianity—without having to necessarily demonize everything they discovered on the way.

What does this "return" mean, however? Few of those who set off along the spiritual path of the East were truly introduced to living Christianity beforehand. In the majority of cases this was not a conscious parting of the ways with "Christianity," let alone a conscious "rejection of Christ," as Christian enthusiasts often like to imagine. What they "abandoned" was often the conventional life of practical materialism, a world in which they mostly never encountered Christianity—but that fact itself argued against Christianity as a possible option: they felt that Christianity had not proved capable of making full use of the opportunities it had enjoyed for centuries in the West. And if they did happen to encounter Christianity, it was more than likely in one of its less convincing guises. Few of those who started to "look in an Eastern direction" did so out of a conviction that Christianity was "bad." Rather they came to the conclusion that it did not "speak" to them.

What are their expectations as they "return" to it—or rather as they look for surroundings in which to encounter it for the first time in one of its more plausible forms? How can we attenuate their possibly utopian expectations? How can we prepare them for the "human factor" in the Church and protect them from the trauma of disappointment—while at the same time showing them what is *the real treasure of faith*, even if we "hold this treasure in earthen vessels"[4]?

People who have experience of paths based particularly on regular meditation usually have no difficulty with any of the ascetic aspects of our faith: self-discipline and an ordered life, that is, those aspects that the very namby-pamby Christianity of our days is selling off bit by bit. What tends to be a stumbling block at the outset is something else: the question of *Christ's uniqueness* and the relationship of Christianity to other religions. Why *not* leave Christ the status of "one of the avatars"? After all, it could be a means of paving the way for boundless tolerance, something that people used to find attractive (and still do by and large) about India's religions. When I am asked similar questions, I tend to avoid catechistic answers (people can study those later) and offer them instead my own, possibly *paradoxical* experience.

I would sum it up as follows: The more I come to know the world's religions and the more I encounter their devotees (in a spirit of "meeting halfway" and striving for unprejudiced understanding), the more I feel rooted in Christ and the Catholic Church.

My feeling of belonging to Christianity is deeper, freer, and more self-evident; it does not need to assert itself by demonizing others. In order to perceive the light of Christ and rejoice over it and in it, I don't need to regard the others as sons of darkness and don the dark glasses of prejudice when looking at them. In like manner, my patriotism does not require me to hate Germans and despise Poles, nor does my proud Europeanism mean I must disparage Asians or Africans.

I recall the liberating moment when I realized that *perspectivism*, that is, the perception that we all look from our own particular limited perspective and fail to see the whole, is no shallow relativism. Truth is a book that none of us has read to the end. That by no means implies that I must regard what is proper to me—*what I see from my standpoint,* my own tradition and my own faith—as less mandatory for myself, or that I must not share my experience or offer it to others. I simply can see no reason why I should look acrimoniously at people who view reality from a different angle.

Yes, I believe that Christ is the fullness of truth, that in him "dwells the fullness of godhood,"[5] and he will never be for me "one of the avatars." But at the same time I know that we each perceive his fullness only to the extent of our human capacity to perceive, and that the Church, "the pillar and foundation of truth,"[6] admittedly received his Revelation in fullness, but there is a difference between the fullness of that Revelation and the historically conditioned forms of its understanding and interpretation. The Church itself as "God's people journeying through history"[7] is maturing to a full knowledge of Christ. Here (in this world at every stage of history) we see only in part, as in a mirror, says the apostle; only when the curtain falls on the historical stage for the last time will we see Him face-to-face.[8]

I reject with absolute firmness the statement so popular nowadays that "all religions are actually the same, and equally valid." No person has the right to make such a bold, and also ludicrously superficial, judgment; those who do so unwittingly set themselves in the position of a god over all. Who could possibly have such a perfect knowledge of "all religions" in order to make such a judgment? Who could compare them all together with such superior detachment?

The more I study religions, the more I am aware, on the contrary, of their *differences*, their variety, their plurality, and their *incomparability*. Each of them is unique. And as my awareness of their diversity grows, so also does my humility and restraint when it comes to expressing any judgment about their validity, even if my intention were to sound good-natured and bring them all down en masse to the same level. They are not the same, and our feeling that they are "similar" stems largely from our badly focused lenses and the poor standard of the telescopes we use to view them. And the question of whether their value is more or less equal (measured in respect of what?), which is "more," which is "less," is—I repeat—a question humans cannot answer. And were believers from many different religions to come together and produce quotations from their holy books to prove that God Himself chose theirs as the only right one, who is to stand in judgment from among the people? Let's leave this task to God alone; let us wait until the Last Judgment instead of playing at it.

The fullness of truth about Christ and the fullness of truth in Christ—which, we believe, are one and the same—truly cannot be seen, let alone "proved" from some would-be independent, objectivist perspective. Only the academic study of religion might perhaps strive for an "objective" perspective—until it discovers that the attainment of that goal is utterly illusory—but this task should certainly not be attempted by theology. Theology must be aware of its setting and its prospects. It is the *hermeneutics of faith*, its intellectual self-reflection; it should not seek to shift from the horizon of faith to some field of fictive "objectivity." So long as theology is aware of and acknowledges this it could even return to the vanguard of the sciences, because many of the latter have yet to make the break from modernity's illusion of "objective knowledge."

The first explicit statement about the divinity of Christ did not emerge from a theologian's study and was not even voted on at one of the famed church councils, but is recorded in the Gospels: I refer to the joyful cry of amazement that escapes from the lips of the apostle Thomas (the "doubting one") when he touches Jesus's wounds.[9] A good number of definitions from our catechisms and theological textbooks are wearing thin after centuries of repetition and now have a stale and musty feel to them. Perhaps they would come to life once more if they were to return to the context of that scene.

I sometimes suggest this very scene as a subject of meditation to those returning from distant spiritual climes and ask them to reflect on where it was, during their journey, that Christ—in any of the guises of his hidden dwelling among us—showed them his wounds, and where they might possibly seek him in future so that the encounter would provoke in them a reaction similar to that of the apostle Thomas's: *My Lord and my God!* When people get a "second wind of faith" it sometimes happens that half-forgotten tenets from catechism classes are once more changed before their eyes into exclamations of joyful amazement.

"Rabboni!" That is another of those cries, this time from the lips of Mary Magdalene, when she realized that the person she was talking to wasn't a gardener.[10] Whenever I read that extract from John's Gospel I cannot help recalling an unsophisticated staging of this scene in an Easter play: the resurrected Jesus was holding a garden rake in his hand and jammed well down onto his forehead was a straw hat, which, to Mary's surprise, he proceeded to remove and toss into the distance with a grand gesture à la Cyrano de Bergerac.

During last Easter I became engrossed more than in previous years in the Gospel accounts of meetings with the resurrected Christ. There is one motif that is repeated several times to striking effect: *They did not recognize him.* For a long time they couldn't recognize him and took him for "a stranger"—and when they did eventually recognize him, it was by signs other than his outward appearance: in his breaking of the bread, from his voice when he addressed them by name, by their touching of his wounds, and so forth.

Maybe the evangelists are thereby seeking to emphasize something about the mystery of the Resurrection: that it is no "resuscitation," no return to the original state, no mere journey back unchanged. Jesus is changed through the experience of death and comes as an Other—a Stranger.

It occurred to me that perhaps these texts are intended to prepare us for the eventuality that not only will Jesus continue to come to us in the forms of his presence that we read about in the catechism, but also looking like a *stranger.* In terms of our own life stories, isn't it the courage to go out and immerse ourselves in what is *foreign* or *different,* and then return, albeit *now different,* changed, transformed, and capable of seeing differently and more fully, that constitutes the participation in the Paschal Mystery, to which we are so fervently invited by Saint Paul, and whose liturgical expression is the celebration of the sacrament of baptism and the Eucharist?

Doesn't it behoove us to set off for some foreign destination "in a distant country" from time to time, so that we may encounter *the other* and—with a cry of joy—recognize anew and more profoundly the closeness of Him who is closer to us than our own hearts? Isn't this time of intermingling cultures and startling foreign incursions, which we often perceive as a crisis of our own values, also *kairos,* a time of opportunity—an invitation from our Lord not to be afraid to enter unfamiliar spaces or to go on journeys, to travel there and back again?

. 9 .

A Rabbit Playing the Violin

On each of my trips to Cambridge, what I have looked forward to most is spending an evening at the home of Professor
Lash—a long after-dinner conversation with the old gentleman by the hearth, with a glass of whisky and pistachio nuts.
Until his recent retirement, Nicholas Lash was the first and only
Roman Catholic among the professors of divinity at that traditionally Anglican university. He is one of the most erudite, wise,
and perceptive people I know. A professor with the reputation
of a very strict examiner and brilliant speaker, he is renowned
for his—typically English—dry, intellectual, and often causti-
cally ironic sense of humor. As they listen to him speaking, his
students and friends are subconsciously waiting for the moment
when, after having allowed his argument to play out in one particular direction, he raises his index finger and pronounces his
characteristic "but." After that "but" everything suddenly goes
off at a completely different tangent and the listener experiences

something akin to what is described in Scripture by the words "the scales fell from their eyes."

Among the few books I have brought with me to the hermitage this year—after my customary process of selection, because I regard the reduction of reading matter to be more of an ascetic exercise than reducing my food intake, and also because fasting is, after all, appropriate in a hermitage—is Lash's latest slim volume,[1] which he gave me at the end of our conversation last April. It was an excellent choice. This witty and extremely insightful little book has transformed the evening hour devoted, according to the rules of the hermitage, to a program of "spiritual reading" into a pleasant and enriching continuation of that spring evening. I look forward the whole day for dusk to fall when I can receive a "visitor from Cambridge" here in the hermitage. Moreover, there is even a hearth here, although there is no fire in it in the summer.

I referred earlier to the way that Christianity allowed itself in the wake of the Enlightenment to be maneuvered into a completely new guise, *and it is precisely this form of modern "religion"—not faith, hope, and love—that is in crisis and coming to an end.* I am grateful above all to Nicholas Lash for this perception. Yes, the moment has come to give the reader a small glimpse of this imaginary evening dialogue in which his ideas—which I heard in our private conversations and have read in his books, particularly this latest one—alternate with how that stimulus resonates with my own reflections.

Professor Lash enjoys quoting an opinion poll about the attitudes of young people conducted recently in the Czech Republic. Only 1 percent of those polled were skinheads, but 8 percent knew what skinheads were and *what they were about.* Only 15 percent of those polled declared themselves to be Christians. However, what was more disturbing was the fact that the proportion of those interviewed who knew what Christianity was and what it was about was also 15 percent.

"At least those young Czechs," says Lash, "seemed to know that they did *not* know what Christianity is about." In Britain everyone would probably say that they knew what Christianity was, but—Lash's typical "but"—we would be surprised to discover how they assessed it and what they imagined it to be.

The point is that a fundamental shift has taken place in the understanding of religion over the past three centuries, and this also includes how the content and sense of basic religious concepts—including the word "God"—are construed.[2] It was not until the seventeenth and eighteenth centuries that the word "God" started to be used *to explain the mechanism whereby the world came into existence.* Previously it would not have occurred to anyone to mix theology and physics in that way. When in the course of the subsequent evolution of scientific knowledge people came to the conclusion that things were rather more complex and that they no longer needed a single external explanatory principle, the discarding of that relatively recent construct—the modern deistic notion of God, which in reality has nothing in common with Christian belief—started to be regarded as "atheism," an abandonment of Christianity.

Another religious concept "pregnant" with atheism, and one that was bound to go nowhere, was the notion that the Christian God is one—the supreme one, admittedly—of a type of "supernatural being," such as gods, angels, and "spirits" in general.

In order to speak of God as a "supernatural being," or to connect God like that in any way with the "supernatural," one has to be an ignoramus who knows nothing about the history of theology or good old Scholastic terminology, Lash grumbles, and adds a charming anecdote as a footnote. "If you come across a rabbit playing Mozart on the violin, you can bet your bottom dollar that the rabbit is acting supernaturally. Rabbits have not got it in them to play the violin. Moreover, things being the way they are with human sinfulness, if you come across human beings acting with consistent kindness, selflessness, and generosity, the same assumption is in order."[3] Such a person's exceptional goodness is clearly the gift of "supernatural grace" from God. According to Thomas Aquinas and the Scholastics, there is nothing "occult" about the "supernatural"; it is simply a kind of *grace*, that is, a gift from God, which extends the "natural" capacities of creatures and takes them beyond their "natural" limits. In short, it is not the outcome of their specific capacity or an expression of their usual quality, but a *gift* (charisma).

In a similar sense, when I scan the pews at the Church of the Most Holy Savior at Sunday evening Mass, I can only surmise who is there for *natural reasons* (by chance or because Halík is more entertaining than the entertainment channel) and whose reasons for being there are *supernatural*—which does not mean they came walking along the surface of the river instead of by public transit, or came in via a closed door, but that they are there on the basis of their *faith*, because, according to the Scholastics, that is a gift of grace, that is, something whereby God extends the natural capacity of human rational cognition. So if we are operating within this scope of Thomist theology, says Nicholas Lash, we cannot, in the case of God, talk about something supernatural, because nothing can conceivably elevate God above His own nature.

It was only when the concept of *nature* altered in the course of the Enlightenment until it encompassed the entire *real world* (which was linked with the naïve notion that we can understand the whole of reality, or that we will soon get to the bottom of it) that the "supernatural" became a dumping ground for everything otherworldly. Not surprisingly, when "God" was to be found in this company of water sprites, fairies, bogeymen, and fairy-tale creatures, sooner or later He had to be banished from the society of rational, educated people and reserved solely for children, the simpleminded, and occultists.

In a typical sentence, Lash declares that "Christians, Jews, Muslims and atheists have this at least in common, that *none* of them believe in gods."[4] They don't believe that such a thing exists, and above all they refuse to worship them.

After the Enlightenment, people believed that religion had to do with belief in specific ("supernatural") entities called gods. Theists were regarded as those who supposed that the class of "gods" had at least one member; "monotheists" were those who maintained that the class had one, and only one member; while atheists were those who were convinced that this class (like the class of unicorns) was actually empty. There are two fatal errors associated with this attitude, Lash maintains. First, the God that Christians, Jews, and Muslims worship is not a member of any class;[5] indeed, by His very nature He cannot be—otherwise He would be an idol. Second, although gods did indeed belong to the world of people since time immemorial, those gods—if we study that word, which in the beginning was not a substantive—did not constitute a separate class of *supernatural beings*, but were simply whatever people worshiped. People did not worship gods; what they worshiped *became* their god or gods. Thus the word "god" did not originally denote any special "supernatural being," but it had a status similar to that of the word "treasure." One cannot go to the market and ask for a loaf of bread, six bananas, two bars of soap, and three treasures. For every individual, "treasure" represents something different; in other words, in its original use the word "god" or "gods" did not denote beings, things, or objects, but *a relationship*.

Professor Lash is an excellent connoisseur and admirer of the works of Thomas Aquinas. He always encourages me to study Saint Thomas and not be put off or misled by what

neo-scholasticism made of Thomas Aquinas when, in opposition
to modern enlightened rationalism, it created its own, competitive, but equally shallow and closed system.

He and I have often talked together about what is possibly the
most familiar part of Aquinas's work, known as the five proofs
of God's existence. In no way can these famous "five ways" of
Saint Thomas be construed as "proofs of God's existence," Lash
maintains; instead, they are a profound and thoroughgoing philosophical meditation about whether the use of the verb "exists"
makes any sense when we talk in terms of "God's existence":
God exists *in a different way* than everything else in His creation
exists. When Aquinas poses the question of God's existence, it
has more in common with the question "Do numbers 'exist'?"
than the question "Do unicorns exist?"[6] Thomas Aquinas is
much closer to "negative theology" than is commonly supposed!

But it was Lash who helped free me somewhat from my
long-standing preoccupation with negative theology and mysticism. He does not like the fact that many theologians and philosophers of my generation share the view that there are actually
two types of theology: "positive" theology full of anthropomorphic and religious notions—suitable for simpleminded people
and popular preaching; and "negative" theology, which negates
all such notions and is appropriate for sages and mystics. This is
nonsense, says Lash; everything we perceive or say about God is
anthropomorphic, that is, inadequate and "too human"—but we
cannot do without it. Otherwise we would have to abandon the
entire "narrative" component of religion and theology. However,
"narration" (particularly the Bible stories) is closer to the depth
of God's mystery than our abstract theological and philosophical
speculations.

Lash does not share postmodern philosophers' aversion to
"grand narrative." On the contrary, the period of globalization—
despite the social and economic difficulties—is one that is

crying out for such a narrative to connect the individual tribal and national experience of hitherto isolated cultures. This cannot be achieved by any ideology, of course, because the path involves a *transformation of religion*, whereby it would free itself from its degenerate modern guise and allow God and the Spirit to enter these newly emerging perspectives—and Lash concludes his latest book on that note.

But first of all, we must realize that the *spirit* is not a spook, "a supernatural phenomenon," or "idea"—but *activity*. After all, Aquinas reflected on whether "God" might not be more appropriately regarded as a *verb* rather than a noun. For Thomas Aquinas, God was not an "object" but *actus purus,* pure behavior or activity! One of the most distinguished British specialists on the work of Saint Thomas Aquinas, the Dominican priest Fergus Kerr, adds: "Thomas' God, anyway, is more like an event than an entity."[7]

In Professor Lash's view, I ought to give up "the philosophy of religion," in favor of philosophical theology. In the British tradition, God, during the modern era, became part of *physics*, as an explanation of how "the world" functioned. In the German tradition, on the other hand, that same period was one in which religion and theology gave way to philosophy and abstract speculation. In the medieval tradition there was no confusion between theology and philosophy: Saint Anselm of Canterbury wrote his *Monologion*, his philosophy (in the form of a monologue), but he called his theology *Proslogion*—dialogue, response-speech. Philosophical theology is utterly dialogical, being thinking based on contemplation, prayer, and reflection.

Professor Lash argues that the situation of Christianity in today's world will not improve until churches are transformed once more into *schools*, schools of lifelong education toward Christian wisdom.

I often tell myself that in the secular world the Church is in a situation not unlike that of the Jewish nation in the Babylonian captivity. The Jews, however, were able to use their experience of the diaspora as a spark to ignite the enormous flame of religious renewal, because in place of the demolished Temple there came into existence synagogues, which were much more like *schools* than churches or temples—schools in which teaching is fundamentally bound up with listening to God's word and with prayer. Out of that blessed change—using a crisis as an opportunity—was born Judaism, in place of the old religion of Israel, and Judaism was to stand the test through all the tribulations of the Jewish nation down the ages and also to have a fundamental influence on the beginnings of Christianity.

Is it possible for us in the Czech lands to expect our churches one day to become lively centers of lifelong education and schools of Christian wisdom? The situation of many churches in our country is sad. They tend to be administered by overworked aging priests who drive from one church to another and have just enough time in each of them to administer the rites quickly to a handful of the remaining faithful who demand it (sometimes simply for very "natural reasons," namely, because "it's always been that way"). And what remains? Don't get me wrong, I have a high regard for the celebration of the Eucharist and equally for those priests; few people "outside" are capable of imagining the degree of loyalty and self-sacrifice of many of them. They not only do as much as they can, but even they do a great deal beyond their "natural capacities"; and "supernatural virtues" truly shine out of some of them (just to qualify that assertion slightly, we should recall Lash's comment about the rabbit playing the violin).

These priests are not to blame for the fate of theology in our country. For almost half a century theology was banished from the universities, and its best teachers were sent off for years to Communist prisons and labor camps. The oldest department of Charles University was replaced by a training college, which the great Czech churchman Josef Zvěřina said, with only slight exaggeration, was more like an "advanced course for ministrants" than an institute of higher education. And then, after it was reunited with the university, the theological faculty languished for several years under the domination of one of the most debased forms of that post- and Counter-Enlightenment vulgarized neo-Thomism. The logical upshot of all that is the sad fact that several generations of priests—unless they acquired additional learning through their own diligence or quirk of fate—were equipped with something that failed to promote their understanding either of the culture of the world into which they were sent or of the depth of the message they were to take to it. So many good, decent, and sometimes very gifted priests were thus condemned to the role of masters of ceremony, who tended to resemble most of all those professional funeral orators at crematoria with their few scripts of platitudes, rather than the prophets and teachers that this country and the Church so dearly need.

"We don't need theologians, we need saints," a certain clergyman once declared to me in superior tones. How far have we sunk, I thought to myself, if we are not ashamed to mouth such empty phrases? And I prayed that the holy doctors and teachers of the Church would forgive him the "mute assumption" that lay behind that sweetly pious cliché, namely, that a fundamental rift exists between sainthood and theology.

Believe me, I have nothing against the saints, including God's saintly simpletons. But I do think that the Lord really has not been stingy to our nation in His supply of *saints* over the past half century. In fact he gave us more than we are capable of appreciating. And interestingly enough, those holy martyrs and professors of the faith, who for years patiently bore shackles for Christ—and are not yet canonized probably because we fail to cherish their memory with sufficient gratitude—include some of our greatest theologians (and our country has never been particularly well endowed with theologians since the days of Matthew of Janow[8] and Vojtěch Ranků[9]); suffice it to mention those priests of blessed memory Antonín Mandl, Jan Evangelista Urban, Dominik Pecka, and Josef Zvěřina.

Wherever I go in Europe I hear that our country is regarded, on the basis of census returns, as the most atheistic country not only of the European Union but possibly of the entire planet. Some of its inhabitants, for some unknown reason, actually acknowledge the fact with a sort of pride.

For some unknown reason? Well, one definite reason is linked with the not so distant past, when several generations of this country's people had it drummed into them that religion is a pack of nonsense. The upshot is that although people don't believe religion to be a pack of nonsense, they regard themselves to be nonreligious and think that "religion does not concern them." The fact that they don't believe in nonsense, if it's true, is a good thing, of course. But the conclusion that is drawn from that is a major error.

I try to explain to people that religion does not solely concern those people who think God exists (and anyway that statement can be construed in all sorts of ways, as has already been said, unless we think hard about what is meant by the word "God" and by the word "exist"), or those "who go to church." We ought not confuse religion with one or other of its possible meanings or aspects and consider it a "worldview" or a "spare time activity."

The sphere of religion, in the broad and basic meaning of the expression, is as fundamental and natural a part of human life as the ethical, the aesthetic, or the erotic, and just as in the case of those areas of life, it can have a different connotation and orientation for specific individuals, and there are different degrees to which it can be cultivated or, alternatively, neglected and undeveloped. The degree to which people cultivate individual areas of their lives depends on many circumstances, and to a large extent on the environment and culture in which they grew up.

Because religious culture was drastically suppressed in this country for so many years—and the ambiguous statement that "religion is a private matter" can be heard once more—this sphere of people's lives is often neglected and choked with the weeds of prejudice and phantasmagoria. Yes, it really is possible to come across people who truly believe in a pack of nonsense, although this category is different from the one that the Marxist-Leninists warned against. Some people still believe in the pack of nonsense that the Marxist-Leninists themselves believed in (or that, in the end, they mostly pretended to believe in), but that type of belief really is dying out. That doesn't mean, however, that various other packages that nowadays constitute "the object of belief" of people who generally describe themselves as "something between" believers and nonbelievers ("I don't believe in God, but there has to be *something* there") do not similarly float on the surface. And one must unfortunately add that many of those who preserved a "traditional faith" (mostly Christian in our particular setting) kept it in such a well-hidden place—out of necessity (because they faced either real persecution or forced isolation from normal free practice of religion, including religious education) or due to wariness and fear—that it "decayed" somewhat. It is therefore not surprising that it is hard to pass it on to others in this form, including to one's own children. The oft repeated assertion that Christianity benefits from persecution is true only to a certain extent; when the Church is squeezed out of public life for too long, there tend to be negative consequences for society as a whole.

Where tradition is interrupted and religious culture undeveloped, various new forms thrive; often they are sacralized and sanctified phenomena of secular society (let us recall the scenes after sports matches). In some cases they assume the form of various kinds of "personality cult," sometimes with comical results, sometimes with tragic consequences. What is happening in Czech society today is not a process of eliminating religion, but instead a process of alienation from a specific type of Christian culture—and the question as to what will step into the abandoned religious field is something that should interest not only church officials.

The widespread opinion that our country and society are nonreligious is used with an odd sort of logic as an argument for the continued marginalization in public life (for example, in the media or in schools) of everything to do with religion, on the grounds that people don't need it, it doesn't interest them, it's superfluous—there is "no market demand." At the same time, however, there exists a sort of intuition that some kind of introduction to world religions is a necessary part of preparation for life in a multicultural global civilization, although this usually comes to nothing because no solution is found to the question "Who is to teach it?" Obviously it can't be an intolerant fundamentalist zealot or a "religious fanatic"—there is general agreement on that—but is it really an ideal situation when the person chosen to introduce young people to the world's religions is a declared outsider with respect to religious traditions? Moreover, in the state of general confusion surrounding religion in this country, it is not uncommon for the label "religious fanatic" to be applied to any believer ("he goes to church every Sunday!").

Many people continue to confuse the desirable religious (or more precisely, denominational) *neutrality of the state* with a certain new type of *state atheism*. If atheism fails to be regarded as one of many "beliefs" and is exalted to the position or role of arbiter on the religious scene, it is capable of being even less tolerant than religion once was in the periods of history when it exercised political power. "Religious neutrality of the state" means a legally guaranteed space for religious freedom and plurality (including legitimate space for people who believe in atheism). Religious neutrality does not exist in a pure form in the case of *individuals*, however: there is simply conscious or unthinking religiosity that can be theistic or nontheistic, dialogical or intolerant, living or extinct, traditional or nontraditional; there is belief in God or His alternatives and substitutes. Just as someone living in consistent celibacy is not "sexless," so also someone asserting his or her distance from all faith is not "nonreligious." Just as the "rejection of politics" is a political stance, so also atheism is a specific religious stance. But atheism also suffered in our country due to the lack of free and objective discussion about religion. It lacks the requisite self-reflection that can come only from a dialogue of partnership.

In our society, religion and religious people are surrounded by a sort of nimbus of strangeness or even eccentricity, above all because of the dearth of reliable knowledge and factual information about religion. As a result, believers find it hard to admit to their faith even in today's atmosphere of absolute religious freedom, and if they do so, or if they are "outed," they often feel obliged to assure the people around them that they are "otherwise normal."

That is also why many young people from our country undergo conversion when they are living abroad, where they are amazed to discover that religiosity, faith, and the Church are regarded as something quite normal. At that moment, what had previously started to form in a vague way within the young person can start to evolve from a "somethingism" or dilettante collage of bits and pieces of different spiritualities and spiritualisms (preferably oriental and exotic) usually into a form closer to European culture and tradition.

Whenever I receive young converts into full communion

with the Church, I often wonder what sort of transformations of "the family of God" these people will experience in the course of their lives. I carefully take note of what is good in our Church and I do not underestimate it. There are also lively parishes in our country and a high standard of church activity, such as in the spheres of charity and education, and there are a number of very capable male and female theologians among the younger generation of priests, members of orders, and laity. And it looks as if the situation might be improving at the theological faculties. I value the witness that many Christians bear to their faith not only by taking their marriage and parental commitments seriously, but even by being ready to accept abandoned or handicapped children into their large families. This is by no means something to be taken for granted in our days, when more and more people want nothing else but to relish the "incredible lightness of being" and lack the courage to start a family and raise children (or rather they lack the values to preserve one, such as patience, self-sacrifice, and fidelity).

Nevertheless, viewed overall, the state of the Church is not too encouraging. In the space of a single generation, the deepening dearth of priests will lead to the collapse of the entire structure of parish administration, and I cannot see sufficient courage or creativity among those who have assumed responsibility for the running of the Church as an institution to find some real alternatives or at least to systematically prepare the community of believers for a situation in which they will soon have to live their faith without the support of many things that the Church has regarded for centuries as essential and matter of course.

Communication between people accustomed to operating within the framework of the Church and the rest of society is in the doldrums, with barricades of prejudice and phobias erected on both sides. In the 1980s, when the Decade of National

Spiritual Renewal first got off the ground, I entertained the hope that the churches could play a significant role in creating a healthier moral climate in Czech society, but these days I am much more reticent in my assessment of the ability of churches to have an effect on society as a whole.

I have also had to shelve many of my former expectations regarding developments on the Czech political scene. I now consider them to have been illusions or wasted opportunities for one reason or another. I do not expect the necessary reform of the political culture to emerge from somewhere—whether from some new political party, or the initiative of intellectuals, or from individual citizens' campaigns. Can one expect something positive in the long term, when a new generation arrives? That's something I don't dare predict.

In the immediate term, the overall state of Czech society and the situation of the churches will probably continue to worsen in many aspects, and it is necessary to prepare for this morally. We must not let any of this break or corrupt us. We must not allow ourselves to be drawn into the murky waters of cynicism, passivity, and bitterness. However, nor must we don the rosy spectacles of illusory optimism. Above all we must reject every kind of drug in the form of ideologies offering simplistic answers or shoddy radical recipes for instant redress. We must simply *stick to the way* and do the best we can and be governed more by our conscience than by circumstances. This will mean, of course, often going it alone against the stream, without any prospects of visible "success" and appearing cockeyed eccentrics in the eyes of the "wise of this world." But should we be unwilling to take this path, doesn't it mean that we have read in vain the gospel of the cross?

The end of modernity is linked with the widely discussed "return of religion." That very expression and the phenomenon it denotes need to be regarded very circumspectly, and it is necessary to distinguish carefully between the two. In one respect the so-called "return of religion" is in no sense a return: religion was always here, is here now, and will probably always be here—and only the ideologists of secularization in the ranks of historians and sociologists are too biased to admit it. On the other hand, one is obliged to note some truly significant shifts and radical changes on the "world religious scene."

Although the concept of "secularization" can no longer be used as a key to understanding the fate of religion, it is also still too early to declare the "end of secularization." Several aspects of what was meant by the term *secularization*, such as the waning influence and sometimes even the collapse of many traditional ecclesiastical forms of Christianity, particularly in a number of European countries, look likely to continue into the foreseeable future.

One reaction to secularization is the many religious revivals, in both the political and spiritual spheres. Some of these "revitalized," or, more accurately, politicized, religions assume militant, impulsive, and fundamentalist forms. An obvious example is radical Islam—a reaction to the ruthless "Westernization" of traditional Islamic society. Another aspect of the same trend is the "Religious Right," which, particularly in the United States, greatly profits from the fear of repoliticized Islam. It is extraordinary to watch how, especially in America these days, radical secularism, on the one hand, and the radical "Religious Right," on the other, demonize each other and whip up a sense of absolute threat within the ranks of their sympathizers. Yet the very survival of Western society depends on the possibility of coexistence and mutual compatibility between Christianity and secularism.[10]

However, as was stated earlier, through their emphasis on "enthusiasm" and "zealousness," some of the "new movements" in the Christian churches, particularly those of the evangelical or

Pentecostal variety, have a tendency to maintain their members in a somewhat infantile or pubertal level of emotional religiosity and to respond to the problems of the world and the churches with simple recipes.[11] I regard them above all as a reaction to secularization. In other words, they are yet another "unwanted child" of modernity that is bound to outlive its progenitor, but the question is whether they offer any truly viable and healthy alternative. The enthusiasm of the new movements is also, of course, a way of giving faith "a second wind" after secularization "took the wind" out of the sails of many Christians. In all events, however, these new movements should not be modern Christianity's only iron in the fire.

As I observe the present situation in the extremely polarized Catholic Church (and I imagine that the situation is very similar in some of the other major churches), I am unable to identify with either of the two extremes of opinion. I do not believe in the least that the solution to the present situation would be a "modernization of the Church" in the form of liberalizing its structures and teachings, that is, "adapting to the present day," as has been called for by many in the media and some movements of Christians in the Church. It has been my deeply held conviction for many years that this is truly not the right path. Although I am in favor of calm and sober discussion of the issues raised by groups of liberal Catholics such as We Are Church, and I believe that on certain matters they are right, I radically oppose the view (which I recognize is not held by all members of that tendency) that democratization and liberalization of the structures, discipline, and certain areas of moral teaching of the Church will usher in a new springtime of Christianity and avert the crisis of the Church. Such an expectation would be just as foolish as the opposite expectations and appeals of the traditionalists for a return to preconciliar triumphalism and the waging of a "cultural war" against the modern world and liberal values. In the first case, the Church would gradually dissolve in the limitless pap of postmodern society and would have nothing to offer. In the second case, the Church would soon turn into a stale sect of backward-looking fuddy-duddies and oddballs: the "cultural war" would be lost before it even started. In both cases Karl Marx's cruel saying that religion is for those who have not yet found themselves, or who have lost themselves again, would most likely come true.

I believe that "modernists" and "traditionalists" alike have simply overestimated the role of the external institutional forms of the Church. Many are bound to go on cleaving to those structures like children clinging onto their mother's apron strings. Many also will continue to wrangle with them like adolescent children with their parents. I must admit I have the greatest sympathy with those believers who treat the institutional aspects of the Church—the "powers that be"—in the way that mature adults treat their aging parents; such a relationship brings more freedom but also entails more responsibility.

I am convinced that the "Church's salvation" will come from neither the Right nor the Left, from neither the past, if we wanted to escape into it, nor the future, if we wanted to plan it according to our notions, nor yet from "above," like a deus ex machina. Positive change can only come from *depth,* from profound theological and spiritual renewal.

In its disputes with Protestantism and modernism in modern times, the Catholic Church placed too great an emphasis on two things: doctrine and authority. Christianity began to look like a *system,* both in the sphere of thinking and in institutional terms. Of course those two aspects are natural and legitimate aspects of the Church and will continue to be so. But my guess is that they will no longer play such a dominant role as hitherto, but will retreat into the shade somewhat. The Church will respond best to the differentiated spiritual needs of the coming generations if it manages to conceive of Christianity *as a lifestyle* whose deep dimension would be spirituality,[12] and its other salient characteristic will be *solidarity*, especially solidarity with those who get a raw deal in their particular society.

Many Christians are concerned that Christianity is losing the clear contours it had in earlier ages and is becoming pluralized. But maybe that weakening of the *system* means in reality that faith is coming *closer to life*, and the undisguised variety of forms means greater scope to address a broader spectrum of people in the future. During the Enlightenment, "religion" started to be regarded as one specific "sector of life" alongside others, and Christianity as one "subsystem" within that concept of religion. Nowadays that concept is considered to be utterly inadequate for understanding the present state of affairs, if not ill conceived from the very outset. There is an effort to find ways of understanding the changes occurring in the relationships among religion, the Church, belief, culture, politics, and society. There is also an attempt to explain the paradox that whereas many "religious structures," which for a long time were the chief interest of those studying religion, are in the throes of various crises, religion as such has by no means undergone the decline and extinction that some predicted, but, on the contrary, has proved to be a more vital, dynamic, and multifaceted phenomenon than could be "explained" by any of the previous theories.

We hold this treasure of faith "in earthen vessels," Saint Paul admits. The Church is a paradox in its passage through history, a paradox between the enormity of the mission entrusted to it, on the one hand, and its fragile, cracked, and, occasionally, dusty and grimy earthenness, on the other. Several members of the clergy have admitted to me that for them the only truly convincing proof of God's existence is that this earthen vessel of the Church—whose fragility they are all too aware of from their own experience—is not completely shattered after two thousand years.

Of course one should not commit the sin of "reckless reliance," which if it were to become habitual—that is, what we call *vice*—could be a candidate for that mysterious and dreadful "sin against the Holy Spirit," which apparently not even the sea of God's mercy can wash away. We cannot just sit back and spout pious phrases. Yes, the "strength of God" is decisive; yet if I understand properly the Paulian paradox, then that strength requires our weakness in order to manifest itself. It can manifest itself in our weakness, but not in our indifference, sloth, bitterness, or cynicism.

We have been entrusted with an immeasurable gift: love, faith, hope. It is our responsibility to protect and cultivate this gift—even in the least favorable conditions. Yes, we are "worthless servants," but our service, which derives from this gift, is necessary and essential. The faithfulness of our service—quixotic and foolish in terms of "the logic of this world"—can be the miracle that opens others' eyes and dislocates that logic. Let us take this task seriously, but let us not take ourselves too seriously: we are, at best, "rabbits playing the violin."

God Knows Why

God knows why the phrase "God knows why" is slowly disappearing from everyday speech. The creeping atheization of our language is an unlikely explanation. After all, one of the most common epithets in the language of today's Czech teenagers is "divine": it can be applied to a rock song, as well as to the singer who performs it, or to some item of clothing. And then there is the somewhat bold assertion bellowed by reveling fans after ice hockey or soccer matches in recent years: "[*Name of player*] isn't human, he's a god!"

Perhaps this is further evidence that our society is not in a state of *dereligionization* at all, but of something quite different, namely: *de-Christianization*. After all, assigning divine attributes to people and things of this world is a typical sign of the opposite of atheism, that is, paganism. If Jews or Christians in this context were to see in that expression of pagan religiosity not just lighthearted exaggeration, but the sin of blasphemy or idolatry, they would earn the reputation of being "a-theists" or "un-believers."

The statement "God knows why" is something quite different, however. It doesn't refer to any god within this world but points beyond the horizon. Whenever something in this world seems mysterious, incomprehensible, or nonsensical to me, this assertion indicates a more distant horizon—albeit one that is mysterious, hidden, and inaccessible to me. I *do not know* (and probably no one does) what is the cause of such things, but they are definitely not entirely without meaning—*God* is the one who knows, and He knows the meaning of everything.

The saying "God knows why" is thus an involuntary confession of faith in the biblical sense of the word, and it is also an act of faith, protecting me from being swamped by events that could overwhelm me with their apparent absurdity. Moreover, it preserves me from pointless speculation and intellectualization; I am able to brush aside many mysteries or accept them as mere chance, because it is not up to me to know everything, let alone perfectly understand or explain it. I can happily live in the vicinity of mystery, because my life is not meaningless, despite all the surprises and enigmas: although *I* don't know the meaning now and do not understand, "God knows why." That's what I rely on and it's quite sufficient for me.

The saying "God knows why" is thus a brief credo of what is sometimes called "collier's faith." A collier needn't know all the fine points of theological argument, yet by his act of faith—an undeveloped faith not based on intellectual reflection—he has a part in the faith of the community of believers.

Several distinguished theologians (and they just happened to be those who were obliged to submit again and again to the Vatican authorities' fresh interpretations of their ideas and statements because of the unwonted depth and novelty of their

utterances about subtle and detailed theological problems) re-
vived in the twentieth century the issue of "collier's faith": the
fact that the Church does not rest solely on theologians, or solely
on the official vehicles of the "teaching order of the Church," but
also and above all on those who overwhelmingly compose it, that
is, people, who know almost nothing about the teachings of the
Church and give no thought to theological matters.

With its enthusiasm for education, the Enlightenment inspired in religion what the theologians of the Church had been
passionately cultivating ever since the time that early Scholas-
ticism borrowed Aristotle's philosophy—trust in the power of
reason—from Arabic scholars. Gradually, however, a major shift
occurred in the understanding of reason—a transition from
intellectus (whose light was a reflection of the light that was
God Himself) to *ratio*, reason as a powerful human tool for the
achievement of success, personal maturity, and the ability not
only to understand, but also to change the world.

In neither religious nor secular matters was it possible to rely
any longer on what "God knows" and the fact that God knows it.
After all, reason was the light that could penetrate everywhere
and radically widen the horizons of what humankind itself can
understand. It can break down barriers forever and penetrate
the mystery that unlettered people formerly respected as the
preserve of Divine Knowledge.

The sheer joy of intellectual adventure—a joy, which once
you have experienced it, and it has become a vital need, you
cannot deprive yourself of it—brought in its wake, however,
something that only a few dared to appreciate absolutely and
express to the full. Whoever seizes a territory that was regarded
as the unique realm of "God knows," becomes a god. No longer
man but god!

This idea was perhaps expressed first and most radically in
modern Europe by Ludwig Feuerbach, who claimed that God

was simply a projection of alienated human capacities that need to be drawn back down from heaven to earth. And that project really was initiated and still continues; a major role in its implementation was played by Feuerbach's pupil Marx and his supporters. And another component of it is the extremely influential current of pop psychoanalysis and existentialist/humanist psychology, which, particularly in the 1960s, achieved a cultural revolution that transformed the climate of Western (chiefly American) society from virtually the very foundations, as well as the style of education and family life, and the spirit of the media. Most recently this unfolding project has focused its attention on medical research and particularly genetic engineering: there we truly do find ourselves on the threshold of the sanctuary of what was known to the Creator of humankind alone, and of which only He was capable.

"Downloading" God's attributes from heaven to earth, putting an end to "divine alienation," and *transplanting the divine into the human ego* also brought about some unplanned and unanticipated changes on earth and in human beings, which somewhat complicated the entire project. After it had received its injection of divine substance, the human ego became rather "outsized," too grandiose by far, and it started to show increasing signs of a spiritual and moral dysfunction rather than a purely mental disorder. The psychologists—as well as the sociologists and philosophers who engage in critical analysis of contemporary Western society—call it *narcissism* or *selfism*. More than a millennium and a half ago, Saint Augustine dubbed it "inordinate love of self." Without the corrective of any divine Thou, the man-god began to suffer from an overgrown ego. Moreover it quickly became so big it somehow didn't fit into its world and started to behave like a bull in a china shop and destroy its surroundings.

During the epoch in which the divine was transplanted into

humans, the saying "God knows" became regarded as something trite, which could be substituted in a nonverbal manner by a shrug of the shoulders. That shrug no longer means that I can dismiss my overanxious questions about the meaning of the mystery because I, in my unknowingness, rely on Divine Knowledge. Instead it is a signal that those very phenomena—and the questions associated with them—are banal and of no significance: they are simply meaningless contingencies. If "God knows why" it happens and it is "God knows what," who is supposed to worry about it? We've more important things to do than think about such stuff, or think at all, for that matter.

Another instance of "collier's faith"? In a sense, yes, but in reverse and with the opposite meaning. Whereas in the first instance it was the unthinking participation of people who didn't have time for philosophical speculation or for a somehow omnipresent religious faith; in the case of today's "colliers" it is unthinking participation in the somehow omnipresent mixture of atheism and paganism.

Nevertheless the light of modern reason did not illuminate everything as thoroughly as it promised at the time of its greatest self-assurance and optimism. The dark corners and chasms of what we don't know tend to be on the increase. I'm not referring to the "still unsolved" problems and enigmas that we can realistically expect humanity to sort out sooner or later with the help of scientific and technological developments. Dietrich Bonhoeffer rightly warned Christians against making the Lord the "God of the gaps," who can be quickly shifted to somewhere that the beam of the light of reason has yet to reach. There is nothing more embarrassing than when Christian faith is associated (and in the worst case when believers themselves associate it) with the dubious band of occultists, esotericists, amateur parapsychologists, spiritualists, healers, and charlatans. They benefit from today's distinctive irrationality-friendly climate, as well as from the aftermath of uncritical adoration of "science" by Marxists and positivists. A justified aversion to the "religion of reason"—something which, on the contrary, ought to unite Christians and respectable members of the scientific community—should not drive them in the direction of the similarly questionable and currently thriving "religion of unreason."

The truly dark and deep chasms of our *unknowing* lie somewhere else entirely, and one of humanity's major moments of disenchantment came when it realized—after the total failure of the naïve optimism of modernity—that no science will fill these chasms with adequate answers, because that is not its mission; in this sphere science is simply not competent.

On the one hand, these are the age-old questions tackled by philosophy and theology, particularly the question of *meaning* in the face of evil, unhappiness, and death; and on the other, there are questions of the moral rectitude of our behavior. These are now particularly topical in those fields where medical science and technology impinge on what is most fragile in the human being, and where the irresponsible application of what we are already capable of (or what we soon will be) could trigger irreversible interference in our humanity and our world.

How many thousands of volumes written on these topics could be summed up—without intending to belittle the efforts of any of us who are involved with these matters—in the words "We don't know"?

I hear an ironical question that provides its own answer: "And God knows?" If He doesn't, what does He matter? If He does, why doesn't He tell us?

We shouldn't let banal questions (or only seemingly banal questions?) provoke us into giving banal answers. The self-assured gesture of evangelical Christians who place a Bible on the table in response is rather tawdry in its theatricality. The old saying "It says it in the Bible so it must be true" is not so easy to apply in this case. We are confronted by a whole set of specific questions that did not confront the people of the Bible, and if we substitute our problems for theirs, and relate answers to other questions to our own problems, then it is not the "Bible itself" that speaks from our words, but instead our all-too-human manipulation of God's word—and such manipulation is unavowed, unthinking, and often simpleminded. Such overuse and ab-use of the Bible is irresponsible not only vis-à-vis Scripture, but also toward those with whom we still have sufficient credit for them to invite us to dialogue and a joint quest.

Yes, a joint quest, that is one possible route. Hard problems such as *how far is it permitted to go* in areas where science and technology open up undreamt of possibilities (and not only in the field of genetics) will not be solved by inspired books, biblical quotations, or decrees of Church authorities; the legislative framework will be established by means of democratic decision making by parliamentary panels, and the actual decisions of individuals will depend on their individual consciences. However, neither democratic machinery nor the consciences of individuals can offer any guarantee of infallibility. There is only one realm that can, to a certain extent, be formed and influenced by the decisions of parliamentarians and individual consciences, and that is the "moral climate" of society, which is a somewhat broader concept than "public opinion" (that other pretender to the throne of infallibility). The moral and spiritual climate of society can cultivate public debate—but again only to a certain extent. That is where believers should be involved, as competent partners respecting the rules of dialogue and conscientiously using all the resources at their disposal: Scripture and reason, tradition and the study of present-day sources of knowledge, awareness of responsibility before God and people, and the thoughtfulness that prayer and meditation confer on human reflection and behavior.

There remains that other area of obscurity that I mentioned, which evokes in us the answer "we don't know," and where we also cannot expect "science" or "progress" to provide the necessary enlightenment. It is the matter of how to retain belief in the meaningfulness of reality and human life in the face of evil, pain, and suffering, particularly in their most extreme forms.

The twentieth century brought frightful waves of suffering, and the first years of this subsequent century promise no improvement. Moreover people's responsiveness to violence and injustice has greatly increased at a time when sources of rapid documented information about these evils, complete with drastic images, have proliferated. As a result, no one can say whether our world is "objectively" worse than the world of our forebears, or whether it is our perception and evaluation of evil that have changed. Anyway that academic question is irrelevant to those who suffer. There is only one thing that interests them: how am I to maintain my personal integrity in the furnace of suffering from which I cannot escape, amid absurd terrorist attacks, natural disasters, and fresh epidemics? It is not only an issue of physical survival—because the fact is that in many such cases this is beyond the individual's control. It is a matter of how to stay sane and not become resigned, where to find the hope and strength to remain in a world like this, and possibly to beget and raise children.

Since time immemorial, the fascinating mystery of evil and suffering has led people to God, but it has also led them away from Him. What is the point of a God who doesn't know what to do about suffering, or if He does, doesn't want to help us? But if we turn our backs on Him, does that do anything to rid us of the suffering, or does it instead deprive us of the strength to confront and cope with evil and suffering?

We can reproach God for not being a mighty golem at our beck and call, assisting us and solving our problems as we see fit. We can reproach Him that He is not on the front line with us in our battles as a mighty arm, clearly visible and at the ready—instead of which He is there only *in the form of hope.*

What is important is the impact of that hope—the extent to which it is a source of strength. Were it to lead believers to sit back and wait passively for assistance from on high, it would have to be rejected. This would clearly be a case of the sin known traditionally as "presumption of God's mercy and forgiveness." It would have been just as much a sin, or an even greater one, if, during the recent tsunami in Asia, people had done nothing but speculate on the extent to which such disasters were God's punishment, and they did nothing to help the victims.

It is despicable to interpret natural disasters in a trivial fashion as expressions of divine wrath and misuse them for the purpose of religious terrorization and reaping "religious capital" out of them. Besides, it is an attitude that smacks of heresy: a distortion of the biblical message about God and creation. The Biblical message of the creation story served to "desacralize nature" and rid natural forces of their demonic or divine aura. Unlike in the mythologies of natural religions, God's wisdom does not dwell in the natural cycles but instead it "found delight in the sons of men."[1]

So let us not go searching in the destructive waves of tsunami for the God we believe in. He is not an irascible and destructive sea god of vengeance and wrath. We can seek and find Him more likely in the waves of solidarity that arose in response to those disasters, whether that solidarity was motivated explicitly by faith or by "ordinary" human love and compassion. "Where charity and love are, there is God" we sing as part of the liturgy for Holy Thursday, on the brink of Easter.

Yes, very many tracts and learned books have been written about the religious interpretation of suffering, and I have read lots of them. Then one finds oneself at the bedside of a child from whose fevered body life is slowly and painfully departing, or with a person whose family has disintegrated because someone else has grievously betrayed their love and trust and caused their world to collapse—and all of a sudden all that bookish wisdom seems like a heavily loaded craft sailing off into the distance. And then not only is one incapable of remembering any of those splendid theories; it even feels as if one's "big faith" has sailed out of sight on that vessel, that clever ready-to-hand faith that has pat answers for every question. All that remains is one's "little faith," stripped naked, trying to find the courage to look into the eyes of the sufferer, in which all one can read is the question "Why?"

But I don't know, oh God, I really don't! And then that little faith does the only thing it knows how to: it takes a deep breath and takes on itself all those questions, painfully open like unhealed wounds, and then, in a single act of trust, it takes a running jump right into the dark gulf of mystery, in which it *does not see* but at least senses hope: *I* don't know, but *You* do!

. 11 .

Living in the Visual Field

I have long been surrounded at home by a whole number of faces that gaze at me from the photographs and pictures beneath the glass on my desktop, or in frames around my computer monitor and on my bookshelves. They include a postcard of El Greco's *Christ* and photographs of my parents and of those who were my teachers—in both an intellectual and a moral sense, such as Jan Patočka and Josef Zvěřina. There are also pictures of some of my favorite saints, and portraits of the thinkers I esteem most and who have been my greatest inspiration. The philosopher Edmund Husserl wrote that our loved ones never really die—we go on sensing them *looking over our shoulders* and approving or disapproving what we are doing. Yes, that's why I have these pictures here: there have been many occasions when I have stood in front of them wondering what advice they would give me in a particular situation, how they would appraise the step I intend to take, or what they would do in my shoes.

To pray means to be aware that *I can be seen*—and maybe the gaze of those many people I am bound to by ties of love and respect assists me in the difficult task of *seeking God's will*. Indeed, my inner dialogue with those people, in whom I feel the nearness of God, sometimes helps me more than leafing through articles of ecclesiastical law or primers in moral theology, although I have no wish to make light of those voices of the Church.

At the time I'm correcting the manuscript of this book, there is noisily obtrusive publicity on both commercial television channels and on the accompanying webcasts for programs modeled on something that once came to my notice on TV screens in Britain and Germany: the *Big Brother* reality show. By means of hidden cameras, viewers are able to watch, at various times of the day, a group of the "elect" chatting, arguing, showering, sleeping, and so forth. The record popularity of the show is partly owing to its "democratic" character: by voting, viewers can influence the participants' decision about who is to drop out of the game, or who is to "survive" and continue to entertain the public until the very end, thus acquiring a horde of fans and a hefty monetary prize.

It is one of those shows that calculates on arousing scandal and protest: its critics are immediately denounced as "heretics"—"elitist intellectuals" and "moralists," who are "detached from reality," and who fail to honor the inviolate rule that "the people want it." They are regarded as a potential threat to democracy because of their lofty conviction that they know what is right.

No, my position is not that of a knee-jerk priggish moralist: the basic *indecency* of this show resides in something of far greater consequence than the fact that viewers occasionally catch sight of the participants' bare backsides or hear the vulgarities used in their tittle-tattle. The real indecency lies in offering viewers the opportunity to be an all-seeing *eye*; that is something that truly does not befit or behoove human beings.

The show significantly bears the title *Big Brother* after the expression "Big Brother is watching you" in Orwell's celebrated vision of totalitarian society, the prophetic nature of which we were able to realize during the period of the Communist police state. The TV reality show is a *different kind of totalitarianism* of course; it is a different way of transforming society into an *animal farm*, to borrow another of George Orwell's expressions.

In the one case it was an attempt by a totalitarian regime to *homogenize* people through external pressure, terrorization, and a combination of violence and propaganda; in the other, the entertainment industry *homogenizes* people thanks to the willing cooperation of those who are prepared to become the puppets of a "big show" in return for popularity and profit. Nevertheless both Big Brothers—the police state and the media creation—are based on the same endeavor to adopt an *all-seeing Godlike position*. It strikes me that the viewers, the producers and the defenders of that show are wrong to regard it as entertainment with a titillating admixture of smut, or as a riveting sociopsychological experiment. These are only secondary aspects; clearly what attracts and entertains the viewer—unwittingly maybe—is playing the role of "invisible witness."

The show is a kind of public liturgy of the substitute religion of a de-Christianized society. On several occasions I have pointed out that I do not consider the main problem of atheism to be "not believing in God," but rather the consequence of that nonbelief—namely, an uncritical readiness to absolutize relative values and play at God. It is characteristic that the stupid TV series in question abounds with pseudoreligious language: the participants are referred to as "the elect"; there is a "confessional"; and so on.

Tomáš Masaryk once urged people to live *"sub specie aeternitatis"*—from the perspective of eternity. Now we are learning to live in the visual field of hidden cameras. Martin Buber regarded God as "the absolute Thou"; these entertainments offer the exact opposite—"the absolute It." The people on the screen become display objects and the people in front of the screen become an anonymous mass, the *quantity* of which serves to silence those who raise the issue of quality. It strikes me as a game, which, in a remarkable way, degrades both its active and its passive participants.

Praying means being aware *I can be seen*. The awareness of living in unhiddenness (as noted earlier, this is an exact translation of the Greek word for "truth") transforms people. But what it fundamentally depends on is the *character* of the gaze to which we are subject. The eye of God is not the lens of an intrusive camera eager to catch us in a comical or titillating situation, in an unguarded moment with "high viewer appeal," nor is it the intimidating eye of the policeman prying into our weaknesses and transgressions of the law.

In general, "it's no big deal" when we commit sins and succumb to our weaknesses. This experience of a "God who doesn't intervene" can be interpreted variously. We can take it to mean that "[God] does not see" or "God doesn't even exist," as Psalm 10 puts it. Another way is to wait anxiously for harsh divine retribution, whether in this life or afterward. Those two attitudes are profoundly connected; many people embrace the belief that "there is no God" with such fervor and relief precisely because they are incapable of imagining God as anything but a cruelly repressive father figure or police official.

In place of those two notions, Christianity offers a different vision, the vision of a merciful and loving God, whose "silence" about our sins need not be interpreted as a sign of His nonexistence, but instead as an expression of His patience and readiness to forgive. But there are also different ways of interpreting a vision of a forgiving God and different ways of reacting to it. We can either turn God into a harmless softy with Whom we can always come to some arrangement, and thereby ease our consciences; or we can experience His forgiveness with liberating joyfulness in the sacrament of reconciliation and respond to His magnanimity and trust by making responsible demands on ourselves, and showing a magnanimous willingness to forgive others.

During several sequences of the *Big Brother* show, I reflected on my experience as a confessor. After all, a confessor is also invited to peep into people's private lives, and people reveal to him what has often remained concealed not only from "the public" but even from their nearest and dearest. But there are many fundamental differences. The eyes and ears of the confessor are not the sensory organs of an anonymous mass of viewers enjoying themselves. The presence of a confessor who listens with understanding to the confession of a brother or sister in the same family of faith, in the same fellowship of "people on a journey," is "anamnesis," a remembrance and symbol of the fact that we do not (nor should we) live our lives as a *monologue*, as a solo performance. After all, we are constantly in the presence of the supremely discreet Other, to whom we can turn with confidence. The confessor is witness to the fact that those who confess do so chiefly before God, to God, and with God. Confession would be worthless were it not preceded by the penitents' quiet dialogue with God within the sanctuary of their own conscience; indeed the Church teaches that what is fundamental occurs in this phase, at the moment of inner conversion, known somewhat clumsily as "the arousal of perfect contrition." If, for physical or moral reasons, it is not possible to confess sins to a priest and obtain his absolution, one can always draw hope of God's forgiveness from having "aroused perfect contrition," that by turning away from evil within ourselves and trusting in God's mercy we allow that mercy truly to enter our lives.

Nietzsche wanted to replace the cold and rigid morality of the "tablets of stone" of unchanging values with "good taste." However, the banalization of life in tune with the ideology of "anything goes"—based on the sole criterion of titillation and *amusement*—not only serves to dull the sense of right and wrong but also engenders a *tastelessness* of a blatant kind. TV shows based on the elimination of intimacy—whether the actors are aware of being "on camera," or, more amusingly, when they forget for a moment and behave with even less restraint than at the moments of the now acceptable level of exhibitionism—are intended as amusement to dispel boredom. However, amusement of this kind has precisely the same effect as any other drug: it deepens dependence, and the addict loses any sense of proportion and demands bigger and stronger doses.

The sacrament of reconciliation, of which "confession" is one component, is not a source of amusement for either the one who confesses or the confessor, but if it is what it ought to be, it can often give rise to a liberating experience of *joy*. Just as hope differs from shallow optimism, so also joy differs from tawdry amusement.

In the world of commercial banality, taboos are only seemingly discarded and suppressed. In reality, strict taboos are erected from beginning to end, particularly around such issues as guilt and moral responsibility. Part of the TV series consists of confrontations between the participants and the TV host in an unwitting parody of "investigative journalism," during which the host asks aggressive and prying questions, which a gentleman—in a culture where "gentleman" is not an empty word and where that kind of public self-disclosure is regarded as a sign of poor taste and ill breeding—would refuse to answer, as being "too personal." Those confrontations are entitled "the confessional."

Those who devise such shows truly have the oddest notions of confession and the sacrament of reconciliation, I think to myself. Would those who feel the need to vomit in public for the amusement of viewers feel a sense of relief if they were to bring their wounds and sordidness into the quiet and safety of a place of prayer and penitence and summon up the real courage to confess, that is, the courage to put aside their masks of "hilarity" and call a spade a spade, and not be afraid to say, "I have sinned," and recognize their fault, determined to take the path of atonement and embrace a change of heart?

Psychology and psychotherapy once extracted one single element—an important one, but not the most important—from that entire process of reconciliation, namely, *confession*, and sometimes they deprived that element of its crucial profundity—the acknowledgment of *fault*, thereby reducing it to a cozy "chat" simply to *verbalize the problem*. The TV "show" then proceeded to trivialize the confession and degrade it into a conversational game in which blame becomes a salable commodity, because it *creates a norm*: thus TV magnates for whom the statement "television does not educate" is inviolable dogma influence viewers in a seductively pedagogical fashion: there is no cause for people to fret over what is joked about in entertainment shows or seek to do something about it: after all, it's *normal*!

It brings to mind a line of Scripture that I am particularly fond of: "Neither shall you allege the example of the many as an excuse for doing wrong."[1]

Among the portraits in my study is one depicting the refined and soulful features of the great British thinker and Catholic convert Cardinal John Henry Newman, the author of a well-known definition of a gentleman, and a man, who, according to the unanimous testimony of his contemporaries, would seem to have been the most distinct embodiment of that ideal of Western—particularly British—civilization.

In Oxford, where Newman taught and where I obtained his portrait, I once came to appreciate—largely thanks to Newman's writing—the original purpose and mission of a university. It was not intended to be an "education factory," in the sense of transmitting information or simply cultivating the thinking process; instead it was meant to be an environment in which the *entire personality was cultivated*, where the scholar became a *gentleman*, that is, someone who, in all circumstances—which need not be favorable to him, and irrespective of whether he is open to others' gaze or alone—remains true to the basic values of the culture he grew up in and for which he bears responsibility.

I realized the enormous contribution that the university had made toward the democratization of European society. Within the university community, the aristocratic ideal was enhanced and became more spiritual (there was greater emphasis on the idea of "noblesse oblige"—that noble birth implies a moral commitment—and the ideal of an "aristocracy of the spiritual" came into being), and it was also *democratized*: in the university community, family origin ceased to be a crucial factor, and even the professional barrier between the clergy and the laity was relativized. University titles became, to a certain degree, the equivalent of aristocratic titles, except that they were not confined to the "highborn" or the sovereign's favorites. In accordance with a tradition formerly observed in certain religious orders, the head of the university, who enjoyed extensive powers, was *elected* by the entire university community, and the university was the means whereby Europe learned that free disputation among the educated was the key to discovering the truth. Many of the positive and important things that occurred on the threshold of the modern age—and which are rightfully acknowledged in the legacy of the Reformation, the Renaissance, and the Enlightenment—emerged from and were inspired by the university milieu.

I am increasingly concerned about the future of democracy. I am convinced that democracy—in both political and economic terms—does not depend solely on the machinery of free competition, but fundamentally relies on a specific cultural context, a specific moral climate, which can boost and strengthen it, but which is incapable of "creating it from nothing" through its mechanisms.

Sir Karl Popper, that outstanding philosopher of rationalism and liberalism, used precisely the example of the commercial media to demonstrate that the principle of free competition need not always result in higher standards: in the specific case of media competition, its tendency is to encourage stupidity and vulgarity.

Doesn't the existence of democracy fundamentally depend on certain civilized prerequisites, on a certain level of education, on motivating citizens to participate in public affairs, and above all on a certain percentage of the population being educated in gentlemanly ideals—on people who observe the rules of *fair play* and respect certain moral principles not out of compunction but because they have a deeply ingrained respect for those values?

Is there no way to prevent democracy—the purpose of which was not least to protect minorities—from being transformed into a "dictatorship of the majority" and what those who run the media declare to be "the majority taste"? Is there no way to prevent a development in which, as G. K. Chesterton once wittily put it, democrats tell the common citizen "you are as good as the Duke of Norfolk," but often they use instead "the meaner democratic formula: 'The Duke of Norfolk is no better than you are.'"

There is no way, of course—not even in the case of the media—of returning to state interventionism or censorship imposed from above. We live in a free society and there is no way of backtracking on the principle of freedom. All the more important, therefore, are measures taken in terms of education and cultivating the social climate in order to forestall the unprecedented onslaught of "neo-barbarism." All the more valuable is every initiative that undermines stereotypical soulless clichés and stimulates critical and creative independent thinking. All the more precious is it when people have the courage to resist the waves of populistic pandering to the lowest values and are not afraid to differentiate and assert certain values at the risk of being labeled as "elitists" seeking to impose their subjective cultural tastes on others. Of course nothing can be imposed, but it needs to be offered. The value choices of each of us are conditioned by our perspective on the world—no one can claim to possess the entire truth—but that does not deprive me of the right and duty to stand by the conclusions I have reached.

It must be the work of Providence that in our milieu, Christians—in common with adherents of many other spiritual schools that are not currently fashionable—find themselves in a situation in which they have no way of supporting their point of view other than by force of argument or personal example. The task of using these sole means of influence properly is therefore an enormous responsibility.

. 12 .

I Cry Out: Violence!

> How long, O Lord? I cry for help
>> but you do not listen!
> I cry out to you, "Violence!"
>> but you do not intervene.
> Why do you let me see ruin;
>> why must I look at misery?
>
> —Habakkuk 1:2–3

I received an invitation to attend the pre-première of an American epic film about the Passion of our Lord, which had already entered the annals of film history by beating box office records in the first weeks following its release. Before the start of the film I cast my eyes around the auditorium.

What stood out most conspicuously in the audience was the vestment of a young priest, who was encircled by a retinue of young women and men, whom he "leads." Whither, I wondered, as I recalled the sort of ideology that had wafted at me from his extensive contribution to the debate at the last vicariate conference, the main topic of which would seem to have been whether it is admissible, acceptable, or forbidden to pray the Rosary with believers during Eucharistic Exposition; the question must have been considered by the assembled clergy as the most burning

issue facing our Church. (I've no idea how this dramatic issue
was solved or whether the assembled priests managed to get to
any other item on the agenda, because after about two hours
of that debate I excused myself on the grounds of some urgent
duty—and it was no lie, because I did truly feel duty-bound to
have a glass of beer in a nearby pub for the sake of my mental
health.)

Seated in the first row at the pre-première, alongside the
journalists and those faces that are never missing when there
is anything that evokes the fragrance of incense, was one of the
gurus of Czech ultraconservatism, who rejects the Vatican of
the last quarter of a century as a modernistic, heresy-riddled den
of the Antichrist. I once read a text by that person, in which he
attacked some Jewish woman artist, belaboring her for both her
Jewishness and her womanhood with such boorish bad man-
ners that as I now perused the features of his puffy face, half
hidden behind dark glasses, I thought to myself that he looked
precisely the way I had imagined him. He, too, was surrounded
by a group of his coreligionists, who were somewhat reminiscent
of the "Friends of Italian Opera" from the film *Some Like It Hot*.
It was truly a bizarre gathering; dear God, would there not be
even one normal man or one normal woman? All these people
were evidently extremely enthused already; after all, this was
their cult movie, so even before it started they were firmly determined they were going to like it. I resolved not to let myself be
driven into the opposite camp too soon.

The film's success had been assured when noisy protests surrounded its first screenings on the grounds of its alleged anti-
Semitism. There are plenty of commodities on the present art
market whose creators desire nothing else than to arouse protest
and scandal, because it is a guarantee of instant media attention and publicity, and that means high attendances and profits.[1]

Our anti-Semite in dark glasses would be disappointed, however. Although the director, Mel Gibson, certainly didn't choose extras with particularly pleasant features for the trial scenes, the film really isn't anti-Semitic, that is, fostering hatred of Jews on *racial* grounds; its overall message is in keeping with the spirit of John's Gospel that reflects the mutual antagonism of the two religions at a time when the early Christian communities were starting to emancipate themselves and demarcate themselves vis-à-vis the synagogues, and events such as the stoning of the deacon Stephen were occurring (and this is reflected symmetrically from the Jewish side in certain passages of the Talmud).

Although I had read much about the film and truly did feel out of sorts in the company that surrounded me (with the exception of a couple of acquaintances in the back seats and one quite normal and truly intelligent and likable young Dominican whom I had gotten to know in the foyer), I strove to keep an open mind. Some of the director's ideas in the film are really excellent; the sets are captivating and most of the actors are very well cast. The atmosphere in the cinema started to thicken when the notorious scenes of scourging—about which we had all read and to which we were subconsciously looking forward with impatience in order to test our mental resilience—finally appeared on screen. And indeed by the end the Savior has been transformed into a bleeding beefsteak, and the director demonstrated that he had dedicated everything he had previously learned in the course of directing almost equally successful bloodthirsty action films, to the greater glory of God and to lacerating the consciences of sinful viewers.

I realized that what I found *offensive* about the film was not the degree of violence; as a confessor I had heard all too often about suffering of this intensity—and particularly of the more harrowing mental variety—so I was unlikely to faint when confronted with pain and blood on the screen. What I found offensive was the film's *Christological heresy.* Our Lord's act of salvation is presented as a *heroic human deed.* Jesus is portrayed in true American style as a champion, excelling in his endurance of pain, one who, in his bout with the devil, is knocked out a thousand times but gets back on his feet again—and at the end worthily mounts the victor's podium. Our Lord's victory and Resurrection is initially hinted at by the frustration of the devil, who tears off his wig in rage, and finally shown through the most banal image of Resurrection: the corpse stirs, folds up the shroud, and walks out of the shot—to audience applause.

What we saw was not the Gospel but a version of *The Dolorous Passion of Our Lord Jesus Christ,* the sadomasochistic fantasy of the visionary Anne Catharine Emmerich, which was a cult work of nineteenth-century Catholic romanticism. I have no doubt that she achieved sainthood through her patient endurance of physical and mental ailments and her life of fasting and prayer, but I see no theological reason why her beatification or canonization should be regarded as some kind of official ecclesiastical endorsement of her visions—unquestionably influenced by her illness—as "direct reportage from Golgotha." The Church takes great care to discourage us from construing someone's canonization as automatic and absolute approbation (let alone universal commendation) of *all* their deeds, ideas, and visions. And that reticence will surprise no one who has done a little exploration into the fascinating realm of the lives of the saints, with all their dramas and paradoxes.

I once assessed a thesis that analyzed over one hundred film portrayals of Jesus's life, from the earliest days of cinematography to the present, and I myself had seen a number of them. It is truly no easy task to attempt to transpose to the screen the multilayered story of the Passion. What is fundamental about the New Testament account is that it contains not one story but four versions, taken from different angles, and none of the mutual tension between them is suppressed. Naïve attempts to harmonize them all and present the Gospel as a fine piece of "documentary reporting," such as Jim Bishop's best seller *The Day Christ Died* or many other similar books, are telling illustrations of how not to treat biblical texts. The Gospels are not documentary accounts by unbiased witnesses, but instead confessions of faith presented in the form of narratives intended, by means of a specific interpretation, to render the "reasons for our hope" accessible to people in ever different environments. Their significance and value have nothing to do with precise photographic details of the external features of those events, but are related to their (often "implicit") *Christology*, that is, appreciating what Christ meant to his disciples and for the world.

Out of all the various "Jesus films," many of which necessarily degenerate into naïve banality whenever they attempt to portray with maximum accuracy "how it really was," the one I actually value most is Martin Scorsese's controversial *The Last Temptation of Christ*, which would indeed be blasphemy if one were to perceive it as a story of "how it really was." But right at the beginning of his film Scorsese clearly states that he is telling a story of "how it really wasn't." His film presents a kind of *negation* of the Gospel story and makes no attempt to retell or illustrate it. It does not relate "reality," but a vision, the "temptation" that is eventually rejected—and for that very reason it provides remarkable stimulus for meditation on the Gospel.

By contrast, those films that purport to be a "cinematization of the Easter events," a would-be attempt at retrospective documentary reportage from Golgotha and a "faithful illustration of the Gospel," in reality portray not the Gospel but the filmmaker and his times. In this respect, however, there are some really interesting "Jesus films": Pasolini's *Gospel According to St. Matthew* reflects the left-wing socially conscious mood of the 1960s, and *Jesus Christ Superstar,* the juvenile counterculture parties of the "flower children"; while *Jesus of Montreal* is a critique of consumer-society hypocrisy and the way the Church adjusts to it. *The Last Temptation of Christ* also belongs in this category, of course, as a kind of provocative postmodern *deconstruction* and "alternative interpretation" of traditional subject matter.

From that perspective, of course, Gibson's film, with all its blood and violence, is also valuable as a testament not only about the director—who is also a Catholic traditionalist and an "action film virtuoso"—but also a *testament to our times*: the "Post-9/11 Era."

Involuntarily, one of the direct eyewitnesses of the events in Manhattan provided me with a valuable key to understanding the phenomenon of terrorism. On the morning of September 11, 2001, she first had a kind of déjà vu experience. It seemed to her as if the world that she acquiesced to every evening on the TV screen along with millions of her fellow Americans—the world of horror films, in which scenes of the collapsing Twin Towers were among the favorites—had become reality and engulfed the rest of reality.

I fear that most Americans managed to mishear the real message of 9/11 and drown it out with the drums of "the war against terrorism" and its quickly fashioned substitute objectives. It seems that few realized that bin Laden was not so much a "wicked Muslim" from a distant Arabian desert as the embodiment of that demon of force and destruction that the American imagination has long flirted with in the form of various King Kongs and other monsters, and which was apparently tamed by the entertainment industry long ago. Now, however, that "shadow" started to behave like the blind Samson whose strength returned with his regrown hair. There was only one European journalist who politely pointed out that bin Laden was brought up and inspired not so much by the Koran as by Hollywood movies. I recalled the very first film I saw as a child. It was called *Revolution in Toyland*. Weren't we now seeing a revolution by that "spirit of horror" that a cocksure society had monkeyed with for so long—starting with the worldwide export of stupid and cruel TV series for children—in its striving to banish boredom and emptiness? Hadn't that hyperrational, success- and power-fixated society been long haunted by a demon of madness and violence that here and there took the fleshly form of homicidal school students—and hadn't it been seeking someone sufficiently exotic to bring this force out of the "collective consciousness," out of the virtual world of TV nursery tales for adults, into the daylight of the streets?

It is not at all my wish to excuse the fanatical or professional killers from the Arab countries or launch a masochistic attack on my own ranks. Yet when the dangerous metaphor of a "war on terrorism" first made its appearance, I was half expecting that a responsible person in America—or the West in general—would utter something similar to the prophetic words of the Czech poet Jan Zahradníček, who just before the onset of Communist gloom wrote:

> *my neighbor, my brother*
> *whoever will paint the world*
> *in the ugly colors of hate*
> *will dip his brush in our hearts as well as his own. . . .*
> *We accuse, but there is a place in the dock for us too.*

The swaggering of idiotic Pentagon generals, with statements along the lines of "We won two world wars and the Cold War and soon we'll win this one," naturally found an enthusiastic

echo among that section of politicians and particularly journalists who love shallow gung ho clichés as much as they love
shouting down "those intellectuals" (and they are past masters at
adopting a tone that transforms that word into an expression of
abuse) who dare to raise critical questions and try to look at the
situation from a slightly different angle instead of joining in the
fireworks of acclamation for the new "Big Brother."

I think that the real "salvation of America" would be fur-
thered much more by thorough self-critical reflection about *the
cult of force and violence* in the country's own culture than by
crusading expeditions into Iraq and other similar operations.
The upshot would have to be much more than a few spirited
articles, however; what is called for is an attempt by those wield-
ing moral and cultural influence to bring about a *change of
course*. There is a need to find ways of at least slightly influenc-
ing the overall social climate for the better, now that Western
society is "spreading globally," and often in its most problematic
guises.

It would be extremely useful if the question "What do they
have against us?," which was voiced so frequently with indigna-
tion after 9/11, could now be posed soberly, and a real effort
made to look at how we are perceived by those distant worlds
and on what manifestations of our culture those perceptions
are based. Do those people have a largely unjust (and often to
us inexplicable) bias against the West? To a certain extent, yes.
But whatever the case, it looks as if that stance symmetrically
matches the bias that most people here have toward them.

Shouldn't we in the West ask ourselves the uncomfortable
question of whether those who have suddenly emerged from
the exotic remoteness of different cultures are not actually setting up a mirror to us? Can't we at least slightly understand the
reasons for the dread and hatred they feel toward us, notwith-

standing those irrational prejudices? Have they not received "from us" something more than our military technology, which we taught some of them to handle expertly when they suited us as allies?

It looks as if so far the forces that don't like complicated questions, that interpret the "war on terrorism" one-dimensionally and are incapable of admitting just how dreadfully they are losing it, still have the upper hand in America. I very much regret that some of its leading representatives use religious and Christian vocabulary to cloak their fondness for simple certainties.

I still await an authentic Christian response to this situation; whenever I hear the hollow clichés of the TV "evangelists" of the Jerry Falwell or Pat Robertson ilk, and of other representatives of the Religious Right and the Moral Majority, I am convinced that theirs cannot be the right way.

The only way viewers can find relief from the stress of the most brutal scenes of scourging in the pious horror film of the "Gospel according to Gibson" is to imagine the buckets of red paint brought from behind the camera by perspiring assistants and the director waving his baseball cap and shouting, "More, more!" But the fact is that those rivers of blood were more authentic than all the rest—the director had not "ladled" them out of the Gospel scenario but out of our common reality, the events *currently taking place* around us.

The director's evident intention was to arouse *feelings of guilt* at the sight of the Savior's blood and open wounds—it was for *my* sins!—leading to *repentance and conversion*. That was also the ambition of the sentimental late-romantic piety, but its roots went much deeper than that. It was the fruit of a certain type of Christian theology and spirituality, and these days such descriptions of the Passion are particularly popular in certain Southern Baptist evangelical circles. I myself once heard a hideous sermon by Billy Graham in which he related how he had urged his children to scourge him because they had been naughty. His intention was to give them a vivid demonstration of how the Savior took upon himself the punishment we deserved for our sins. (I couldn't help recalling a sketch at the Jára Cimrman satirical theater in Prague in which the schoolmaster says to his class, "You've been so naughty today, children, I'm not going to smoke my usual cheroot. Don't cry, it's all your own fault!")

And it's a fact: hundreds of conversions were announced throughout America ("Americans enjoy converting several times a day," one of my colleagues said with a smile), and clergy from all denominations (including some Catholic convents, alas) ordered copies of the film in bulk.

But is this a way to treat the Easter mystery? Was that truly the reason that Jesus took upon himself the cross and why Paul presented to the world the message of the cross and the Resurrection as a key moment in the history of the entire cosmos? Is that the mystery we proclaim every time we celebrate the Eucharist, saying, "Christ has died, Christ is risen, Christ will come again," and we "make the memorial of his Passion"?

Isn't this instead a regression to pre-Christian times—not so much to the catharsis of the ancient Greek tragedies as to the orgiastic goings-on in the Roman arena or a reversion to a world of blood sacrifice—the world that was supposed to end for good when the angel stayed Abraham's hand above Isaac's neck?

When I read about the Easter Passion to the assembly of believers or walk the stations of the cross with them in meditation, I have no wish either to manipulate them into the role of Christ's tormentors in order to "soften them up" or to touch their heartstrings to evoke the emotional effusions of the weepers of Jerusalem—who, according to the Gospels, were rebuked by Jesus himself on his way to crucifixion. Provoking emotional torrents by means of cheap effects risks not opening up but barring the path that the Easter message invites us to embark on. Yes, of course it is a path along which we are guided by our "hearts," but in its biblical sense the heart signifies not emotions and sentimentality but a deeper understanding.

Gibson's film is possibly a useful antidote to excessively abstract and polished sermons, in which the actual story of the Passion almost gets lost amid hyperintellectualized and hyper-contrived theological schemata. Every Catholic is bound to have heard tell of Anselm's economic and legal theory of redemption as ransom paid to Satan, who, after Adam's sin, acquired legal power over humanity, or his explanation of commensurate compensation for the affront to God. Maybe the medieval passion plays and the cult of the Precious Blood that Gibson undoubtedly draws on were some kind of subconscious protest against such excessively abstract theological/economic constructs and an attempt to draw attention back to the raw narrative.

However, Gibson's attempt at retelling the story founders precisely at the point where the director "caught the scent of blood" and allowed himself to be so possessed by the magic of violence that he completely "dropped out of the story" (or at least so it seemed to me) and landed where? In our own times.

Films of the "Passion of Christ" variety are also trying to be (and indeed are) a *sermon* of sorts. A sermon is supposed to "build bridges" between the scriptural text and our experience of the world. It is supposed to promote a *hermeneutical circle* in which the Bible and our life interpret each other, so to speak. But what remained of the Easter message in that film? Just streams of blood, a hero who endured everything, and a resuscitated body at the ending. What does that say about Christ—and what prospects does it hold out for our world, which is overwhelmed with violence?

When I first heard comments from Buddhists (and even from someone as wise and erudite as Suzuki) that Christianity has a fascination with violence and places the hideousness of suffering on a pedestal, a place they reserve for their calmly smiling Buddha, I had the feeling that in this matter the East demonstrates a profound misunderstanding of us Christians and our symbols. When I first heard about the protests of parents in Bavaria demanding the removal of crucifixes from schools because their children were being forced to look at such a dreadful spectacle, I just could not believe how people brought up in a culture saturated with Christianity could totally fail to understand the message of the cross.

After all, Christianity truly *does not glorify violence*! It simply does not censor the reality that violence is part and parcel of our world and our Lord was not spared it. But it also says that *violence does not have and must not have the last word*, that Jesus preferred to allow himself to be killed through violence, rather than use or condone violence. Christian belief states that after Christ took violence upon himself, violence no longer existed as a harrowing absurdity, but underwent an inner transformation, by the meaning that Christ gave his suffering and death. The cross is not a "demonstration" of violence, suffering, and death; on the contrary, it is a message about a love that is "stronger than death." It preaches the strength of hope that relativizes and mocks death itself: "Where, O death, is your victory? Where, O death, is your sting?"

One cannot distort the significance of the cross in this way and wrest this symbol out of its context! The Gospel does not relate the story of the cross as a horror story in which suffering and horror are an end in themselves, where they are a means of achieving a pleasant nervous thrill. The image of the cross and suffering points to a broader horizon—and that's what it's all about!

As I watched Gibson's film I had the impression that the cross, suffering, and blood had assumed center stage to such an extent that they ceased to point toward the wider context and horizon of the Easter message and instead they obscured it. I said to myself nevertheless: Wasn't the film precisely for that reason involuntarily a profound statement about *our* times, when violence is fascinating because it is an end in itself and no longer points anywhere else but to itself?

Violent death is always a terrible thing, but executions and wars, for all their horrors, at least had a specific purpose. Air raids on enemy territory, with many predictable civilian casualties, admittedly broke through certain barriers in the history of killing, but these campaigns too had some kind of logic—albeit hard to justify; there was still a distinction between the front line of the war, our territory, and the territory of the enemy. But because of suicide bombers who place explosives in busy locations of international cities where *anyone* at all—including their political comrades and fellow believers, as well as their compatriots and their wives and children—might pass by, *the entire world is now enemy territory.* What sort of paradise do they think they'll wake up into, the people who create hell on earth through this perversion of the tradition of martyrdom? In 2004, terrorists chose a school as their target and schoolchildren as their hostages. If the word "diabolical" still retains any meaning for us, then I think we need not have scruples about applying it to such acts.

"Demonic" is the opposite of "holy," and let us not forget it! A few years ago I read a remarkable study about the fascination of violence and the genesis of sadism; it was an essay on the work of the Marquis de Sade. The author pointed to the fact that when, during the Enlightenment, religion was identified with the sphere of "the rational and moral," the *holy* or *numinous*, that *mysterium tremendum et fascinans*, which makes reason dizzy, retreated into two bolt-holes: violence and sexuality.

Maybe this detached view will help us understand why sex and violence are central to the stories that are poured into the subconscious of millions of people in our civilization night after night by means of suggestive images, and tricks of cinematography and computer technology. People who have otherwise lost touch with the numinous subconsciously sense here a possibility of stepping outside the sphere of the rational and thereby obtaining a little bit of ecstasy and an escape from the monotony of their daily lives. Take a good look sometime into the eyes of children who spend hours every day in the peculiar mental masturbation involved in computer games that allow them to experience the delight of killing "as a dry run"!

The pressure of the mundane, the threat of the stereotype and of boredom, the experience that everything will quickly pall—all encourage the escalation of experiments and the transgression ad absurdum of what were only yesterday indisputable boundaries. And the moment comes when the game crosses the boundary of the mere game: the thrill of killing, experienced a thousand times over for fun in computer games or when gawping breathlessly at horror or action movies, breaks loose from the world of overexcited fantasy and spills across the now undefinable frontier between the virtual and the real. Violence dances in the school and in the street, drawing everyone into the game. Killer and victim are interchangeable roles that can even be combined quite easily. *Anything goes!*

No, I have no panacea for the pain of violence. I bring this wound of our world into my meditations on the stations of the cross. Yes, from time to time, when I close my eyes during this time of prayer, the alluring and obtrusively performed scenes of violence from Gibson's film come back to mind. No, the Jesus I believe in is not a Hollywood hero; he is not a champion in the suffering stakes. His resurrection cannot be captured by the camera's eye. It takes place at a much deeper level, at that indestructible layer of reality called hope.

The German poet Georg Büchner called suffering "the rock of atheism." When confronted with suffering, many people have concluded that the "hypothesis of God" must be erased from their perspective on the world. All right, let's erase it, but does that do anything to reduce the degree of suffering in the world? Or doesn't it rather reduce the power of hope and thus give evil an opportunity not only to triumph in the external world but even to blight the human heart with cynicism and despair?

Faith, which can be humanity's ally in the fight against the evil of violence and against suffering and cynicism, must not churn out tawdry explanations; it must radiate hope.

Hope is the gift that God gave His creation; it is the ability to perceive reality as permanently open-ended.

The stations of the cross end at the point where the One who did not shrink from the forces of violence and death is laid in the bosom of his mother and then in the bosom of the earth. But Mary, who believed that "nothing is impossible with God," remains a beacon of hope even at that moment of darkness: contrary to all expectations, even at this moment she believes that God has not yet said His last word.

Many modern depictions of the stations of the cross append to the classical fourteen scenes a fifteenth scene of the Resurrection as a final station. I personally prefer the classical version, which indicates that we are still "in mid-story," that the

Resurrection is not simply the next station but is instead a different dimension that we can enter only in the mode of hope. Nevertheless, it is precisely that hope that is the key to understanding the story as a whole.

When we eventually learn to relate the Easter story not as a gory tale to arouse feelings of guilt, but in such a way that the infectious power of hope will be apparent from our preaching, then people will not feel obliged to remove crucifixes from their walls, because they will understand the message. When we eventually learn to *live* that message in a credible way, then violence—both the cinematic and the real kind—will not be permitted or able *to have the last word.*

The Sign of Jonah

"Pope John Paul II Is Dead." It is a Monday morning and I am sitting in a plane to London reading over and over again this title on the front pages of all the newspapers on the seat next to me. It happened on Saturday evening, and since then I have heard the news and various commentaries many times already, but here, for the first time, I see the sentence written "in black and white"—and I try to be simply a mute observer of the wave of feelings, memories, and associations that wells up within me at the sight of these words.

I first spoke his name in the Eucharistic canon when I celebrated my first Mass. It was seven o'clock in the morning behind the closed doors of the choir chapel of the Ursuline convent in Erfurt, following my secret ordination to the priesthood. I was not the only one for whom the name had a "fresh scent": it was just after the surprising election of the "Pope from the East." Yes, I was most likely the first priest in the entire Catholic Church to be ordained during his pontificate. When my *prima missa* was finished I went with the bishop to watch the television coverage of the solemn inauguration of the new head of the Church.

It was a new name, a new face, and also a new spirit—the pope's first sermon *"Be not afraid!"* was an urgent and energetic challenge, and not only to the world's billion Roman Catholics. For a newly ordained priest who was due to return to a police state in a couple of hours' time to start his priestly mission "underground," and who was trying not to think about the risks and hazards of this new phase of his life, which had no known or foreseeable end, those words had the sound of a very personal message.

At every Mass for the next sixteen years and more—often every day, in other words—I spoke the name of *our Pope John Paul*, and that name became closer and dearer to me with the passage of time. After November 1989 it acquired an even more intimate flavor and aroused the memory of my first meeting with that man on the eve of the fall of the Berlin Wall. And then, in the subsequent years, there began to accumulate in my memory traces of more and more meetings and conversations in the refectory whose window shines onto the square in front of St. Peter's Basilica. The name thus accompanied me over the course of my life as a priest, which at that moment was precisely as long as his lengthy pontificate. He was for me not simply "our Pope John Paul," as everyone called him in the Eucharistic canon, but also *my* pope, who had a unique emotional connection with my own life story, my faith, and my hopes. Yesterday, Sunday, I first celebrated Mass without speaking his name—and at that moment of silence in the canon my heart missed a beat, and although I tried hard not to show it, my voice broke as if something had died within me.

I can remember all the great moments of his pontificate. The news stories about them, which at first reached us—with great difficulty and belatedly—after penetrating the barrier of ideological censorship, were to become louder and louder signals of encouragement: the pope standing in the square in Warsaw and on the meadow below Kraków amid throngs of millions. It was Pentecost 1979, a real Pentecost: the pope spoke in a language that everyone suddenly understood, a language of freedom and hope, while the Newspeak and Ptydepe[1] of Communist propaganda have since then been forgotten and wafted away like a stale smell from a room where someone has finally opened wide the windows after many years. I recall the stories of my German friends about his first visit to their homeland. The liberal Catholics with their categorically critical attitude to the representatives of ecclesiastical authority—an attitude I could not understand at all at the time and which therefore deeply offended me—were evidence of how, when experienced at close quarters, the pope won people over with his sincerity and conviction. I can also remember how eagerly I read, with a sense of agreement and concurrence, his brilliant speeches to European intellectuals—in Germany at the tomb of Albert the Great and in Paris to the UNESCO General Assembly—speeches that I read in well-thumbed copies of samizdat editions distributed secretly among goodness knows how many readers. I shall never forget the effect on me of the photograph of the first meeting of representatives of world religions at Assisi, when I first set my eyes on it in a smuggled magazine in a meadow not far from the town of Počátky: the pope holding hands with the Dalai Lama, the grand mufti, and the chief rabbi. I was aware with gratitude that I had been permitted to be a contemporary of enormous groundbreaking events that no one will ever erase from the memory of the human species—moments when locked gates were opened after a thousand years and no one would close them again.

But I also remember how hurt I was at that time by the

criticisms that started to be heaped on the pope's head during those years—from both sides of the Church—after the international public's initial enchantment had cooled. For one section of the Church he went too far (particularly in respect to embracing other religions) and for another he was a reactionary.

In 1989 my life, my priestly ministry, and my vision of the world were drawn into a new context and the horizons of my experience were radically broadened. As a result of that new experience my enthusiastic and devoted attitude to the Church was also tempered by certain feelings of disappointment and hurt. I started to understand how people living in freedom have a greater capacity to perceive reality from more than one angle, and hence be more critical toward their own Church and its representatives than those who inhabit a besieged fortress, who subconsciously resist anything that might undermine their combat morale. I was gradually forced to admit just how much we, the determined opponents of Communism, had been damaged by our immersion in the envenomed atmosphere of a totalitarian society, a climate that ultimately afflicts the rulers and the ruled. I learned—and am still learning—patience, the art of waiting until—perhaps with the arrival of a new generation—the wounds and paralysis of society and the Church will slowly heal on the ruins of the bureaucratic and police-ridden empire of world Communism.

I would frequently go back to the pope's analysis of the spiritual and moral dilemmas of a world in coalescence after the collapse of the bipolar system: his encyclical *Centesimus annus*, and particularly the passages about *human and social ecology*, where he writes about the need to care for the social and cultural structures of the environment, which are vital for the truly healthy formation of a mature personality. It irritated me that with their fascination with a limited range of issues, dominated always by anything to do with sex, the media blatantly diverted the public's attention away from these pivotal ideas of John Paul II to an entirely marginal agenda, and they even caricatured and trivialized that part of his message, ripping it out of the context of his theological anthropology. In the mask of "the conservative from the East," which not only the gutter press but also a number of reputable intellectual commentators strove systematically to force onto Karol Wojtyła, I did not recognize the features of the man whose texts I had carefully studied and with whom I had had repeated opportunities to converse in person. One of the BBC commentators, bowled over by the planetary response to the pope's death, particularly the reaction of young people, said to me at a rare moment of critical self-reflection: "It seems to me we got him completely wrong; we didn't understand him."

Over the years, one theme began to appear with increasing frequency in his writings, one that seemed to be his "idée fixe." That theme was *the significance of the year 2000.* The pope had called the reforming Second Vatican Council "a providential event" preparing the way for the celebration of the new millennium, and his own pontificate as the "vigil of the jubilee year." He gave an increasingly reasoned theological and spiritual dimension to the idea of celebrations of this symbolic anniversary of Christ's entry into history. He drew inspiration from the Old Testament understanding of jubilee years as a time of reconciliation, penance, and purification. He requested from the Church and from "all people of goodwill" that they should make thorough preparation for the great historical opportunity and not waste it. He linked with the idea of the holy year possibly the greatest moral deed of his pontificate, the memorable "Mea Culpa"—his public acknowledgment of the Church's historical faults and failures and his plea for forgiveness on the eve of Lent in 2000. Rightly he started to be nicknamed "the pope of the millennium."

The year 2000 came and went: what happened? Weren't

the pope's expectations simply a foolish dream, a wish that did not come true? Didn't his exhortation for a conversion of hearts evaporate? Wasn't it drowned out by fatuous triumphal parades or by stereotypical "down-to-earth" thinking that ignores all the magic of the jubilee, seeing it as an artificial human convention of dubious significance?

If we look at the events of the first years of the new millennium it is truly hard to identify any striking "fruits of conversion." What is evident at first glance is the alarming surge of international terrorism, the unfortunate war in Iraq with its many tragic consequences, and natural disasters of unprecedented proportions. There is also not much to be heard about the "new spring of the Church," and the "new evangelization of Europe," which the pope constantly proclaimed, is gradually taking the form of mindlessly repeated phrases culled from Church documents but has not manifested itself in the life of our continent.

When I was almost on the verge of falling prey to total skepticism after looking beyond the gates of the new millennium, I was struck by the Gospel passage: "no sign will be given it [this generation] except the sign of Jonah the prophet."[2]

The book of the prophet Jonah is among my favorite texts, above all because of the subtle humor and irony with which the Lord treats his chosen, though not entirely successful messenger. By referring to Jonah's story, Jesus evidently seems to have been saying that, as in the case described in that book, where people received no other sign than the person of the prophet and his words, so now also people ought not to be on the lookout for extraordinary, external "proofs" but should open themselves to Christ and his message. But let us remember the dénouement of the book of Jonah: after the prophet's preaching, after his passionate predictions of disasters, *nothing happened*—as a result of which the prophet is utterly frustrated and bitterly reproaches the Lord for having shamed and discredited him.[3] But the Lord's apparent inaction actually conceals something, which, from the prophet's standpoint and any position of "detachment," could not be evident: a profound change of heart has occurred among the Ninevans and the Lord has let the city remain on the surface of the earth.

When, on the eve of the new millennium, I was asked by journalists where I saw hope for the future, an utterly simple answer occurred to me: the fact that we are still here. During the twentieth century humanity acquired unprecedented means to wipe itself out quickly, totally, and for good. Seldom in previous ages—although it is hard to judge this "objectively"—had so many madmen and hate-ridden ideologies appeared on the historical stage and received such a massive response that millions were willing to let themselves be beguiled by the spiritual opiates of national, racial, or class malice. Yet we did not destroy ourselves; yet we are still here.

There are many possible explanations, ranging from facile answers ("lucky chance") to the complex theories of historians. But can we simply throw overboard the old belief, nurtured in the heart of the people of the Old Testament, that the existence of a certain number of *hidden righteous people* is what holds the world together?

Didn't the old man on the throne of Peter—and maybe quite a number of those beyond the bounds of the Church who did not spurn his challenge to conversion—belong to that handful of the righteous, on whom the existence and still open future of our world depends? "Nothing happened," agreed, but isn't that fact precisely "the sign of Jonah"?

To mark the year of the millennium I wrote a not particularly successful article entitled "The Pope and His Year." I did not suspect at the time that the real "year of the pope" would not occur until five years later—the year of his death. For several days something blew through the world that swept away, like so many scraps of paper, all the journalistic clichés about a reactionary pope attached to "outdated dogmas." For a moment the world stood on tiptoe in silent suspense: everyone suddenly realized that a great—truly great—man had passed away.

"Is that infirm, drooling old man in a wheelchair really a representative image of your Church?" That is a question I was asked several times in recent years. "In a certain sense, yes," I would reply. "If you look at the outward appearance there's much that is lamentable about it. But if you manage to look deeper, you'll find a strength similar to that of the ailing pope."

No, I was not ashamed of his physical frailty. I was glad that in him the Church had a different kind of representative than "this world" has on offer, with its stereotypical assortment of sexy and sporty politicians and leaders—mannequins groomed according to the dictates of TV ads to be eternally young. I was glad that this pope sent out a message to our ever more rapidly aging world that age is no reason for consigning a man to a depository of redundant material.

Now that he has carried the cross of his ministry to the very end, many things have become clear. It emerges that he did not perceive his papacy as a job with a time limit but as the mission of a *father* that naturally cannot end by "retirement." Dear children, I am seventy years old, find yourselves a younger daddy! (Is it really true, that mindlessly repeated phrase that modern mankind is adult and needs no paternal authority in public life?)

Yes, his ministry was also summed up in that "final sermon"—the helpless croaking and the waving from the window followed by the peaceful and dignified dying before the world's gaze.

My colleague Václav Bělohradský, who has seldom had many nice things to say about the Church, wrote some splendid lines about that "last sermon," that wordless gesture that numbered the pope among the myriads in our world who "have no voice." Bělohradský admitted that it was a moment when he envied the Catholics their pope.

In Cambridge, during an academic conference, I watched television coverage of the pope's funeral together with a group of sociologists, political scientists, and theologians of various denominations and from different corners of the globe. The television reporters repeated endlessly that this was probably the biggest funeral in history. The coverage was punctuated by reactions from individuals from all continents, who were evidently sincerely moved by the event. One of my colleagues said quietly: "This is a phenomenon that forces us to look at the place of religion and the church in our culture with fresh eyes and in a different way: something has changed."

Yes, something has changed. The feedback sections of Czech Internet newspapers, where the slightest positive comment about Catholicism usually arouses absolute geysers of blind and frenzied hatred and vulgarity, gushing from dark corners of the soul, are today silent, as if someone had clapped muzzles on those spiteful scalawags. The occasional shrieks of blasphemy fall on such deaf ears that their originators could well stop for a moment and consider just how lamentable their attacks are. The television announcers wear black ties and speak in grave tones about "the Holy Father." Yes, I know it is just playacting—tomorrow or the day after they will be bawled out for hamming it up—and the media—for the sake of balance—will set in motion, with renewed vehemence, the tumultuous remonstration against the dreadful Church that refuses abortions, euthanasia, cloning, artificial contraception, homosexual marriages, and all the other wares on the global market.

It's odd how the advocates of extreme libertinism, who dominate almost all the most powerful mass media and who usually invite representatives of other shades of opinion chiefly to play the role of the dull-witted Dr. Watson, whose naïveté serves to accentuate Holmes's perspicacity, are so keen to have the Church and the pope applaud their views. Can't they simply brush aside what the pope has to say about those issues? And would they (or the Church) really want the sort of pope who would betray his mission and his tradition, one who would simply mimic obediently everything that they have already been trumpeting—much more powerfully and loudly—to the entire world? Could such a pope command their respect? Or could it be that somewhere deep in their souls and consciences they are not entirely convinced about the truths they proclaim with such assurance, so that they feel the need to shout down or ridicule this almost lone voice, who in the midst of our Western culture says something different, who quietly and perseveringly offers people the opportunity to reflect on whether the slogans of libertinism are truly so infallible as they purport to be?

It's odd how the historical roles have been transformed. The papacy, which has long since had no political or coercive power at its disposal, nor, for that matter, any power other than the moral influence of the word issuing from the lips of a *pilgrim*, tirelessly addressing the nations, has nevertheless become a force that no one can ignore. In the brief "closed season" for Catholicism—the few days between the pope's death and his burial—the world's media are pronouncing a surprising truth: during the incumbency of John Paul II the authority of the papacy seems to have been greater than at any point in its entire 2,000-year history.

"The most conspicuous man in the world of the last quarter of the twentieth century has died," says the man on the television screen. It seems that the pope is beginning to be missed even by those who roundly disagreed with him in many respects.

On Friday, the day of the funeral, I received a surprising invitation from one of my Cambridge colleagues, a believing Jew, to join his family and friends at his home, in the supper that marks the start of the Sabbath. I arrived at the house on the edge of town to find a table ceremoniously laid, on which there stood a candlestick and wineglasses. The opening prayer of Psalms concludes with the peace greeting "Shabbat shalom!" And on the bookshelf there stood a single picture—a photograph from the front page of today's issue of the Jewish religious bulletin: the pope leaning his forehead against the Wailing Wall in Jerusalem. During prayers, his name is recalled, and he is the sole topic of conversation throughout the supper. One of the people attending the supper said to me afterward: "Even if you Catholics were to forget about this pope one day, the Jewish nation will never forget him. For us, he will always have a prominent place as one of the *righteous among the nations.*"

Pope John Paul II has died. There is silence—almost the silence of Holy Saturday. The bells of St. Peter's Basilica chime out over a strangely silent motley throng at midday, when the wind, which has for some time already been flicking over the pages of the Gospel placed on the coffin, suddenly closes the book.

. 14 .

The Prayer of That Evening

Before we set off this evening[1] for the place where we are to pray together as Christians, Jews, and Muslims for the future of Europe, I would like to relate a Hassidic story to you:

Rabbi Pinchas asked his students how one recognizes the moment when night ends and day begins. "Is it the moment that it is light enough to tell a dog from a sheep?" one of the pupils asked. "No," the rabbi answered. "Is it the moment when we can tell a date palm from a fig tree?" the second asked. "No, that's not it, either," the rabbi replied. "So when does morning come, then?" the pupils asked. "It's the moment when we look into the face of any person and recognize them as our brother or sister," Rabbi Pinchas said. "Until we're able to do that, it's still night."

It was a long night during which we, the children of Abraham, believing in one and the same Almighty God, were unable to recognize and acknowledge one another as brothers and sisters. It was a long night of mutual fear, prejudice, and hatred, a terrible night of history, in which our ancestors and predecessors wounded each other, and those wounds have not fully healed and still cause pain. Thank God that in the past there have also been sublime moments of peace, and that in each of our spiritual families God awakened, at various periods, individuals whose hearts and minds were so open that they sought the paths of reconciliation and of understanding for others, even though they frequently suffered injustice from their own and their nearest. Let us remember them and offer thanks to God for them as we walk through this evening's darkness, so that we may prepare by common prayer for a dawn of reconciliation and a new beginning.

Long before his own brilliant mind was clouded by madness, that great prophet of the period of European nihilism, Friedrich Nietzsche, narrated a parable about the madman who came with a lantern in the daytime among people who no longer believed in God, and asked them the question: *Where is God gone?* Unlike them, he knew the answer: we have killed Him. He came with a lantern because unlike them, he was aware of the night that the earth had been plunged into after that event—"far away from all suns."

In another work, Nietzsche wrote that nihilism, that least welcome of all guests, already stands at our door. But for Nietzsche, nihilism, like the death of God, was ambivalent—a threat and an opportunity at one and the same time. In the twentieth century, on the threshold of which the prophet of God's death died, nihilism entered the European home by the front door. It was the beginning of a deep night in which the children of Abraham, who for so long had killed each other, were murdered en masse by those who believed that the God of Abraham—not just the God of the metaphysicians, which

Nietzsche had in mind—was dead and must remain dead. The genocide of the Armenians, the Shoah of the Jewish nation, the suffering of millions of Christians in the concentration camps of Nazism and Communism, the massacre of the Muslims in Kosovo . . . How much suffering was endured by the people of the land where we meet today, and how many others suffered on Polish soil when it was under the enemy yoke!

But hope and opportunity are concealed within even the deepest and most painful night. John of the Cross, a great mystic of a country in which Christians, Jews, and Muslims lived and contemplated together, wrote a lot about the significance of darkness for man's relation to God. The dark night of the spirit, in which people are confronted with God's silence and feel the absence of God, is an extremely important time for a person's spiritual growth and maturation.

Might it not be that that time of horror, when God seemed to many to be silent or absent, and when many thought Him to be dead—that *collective dark night of the spirit*—was a key moment in history, which will only now show forth its fruits?

"But where danger threatens, that which saves from it also grows,"[2] wrote Hölderlin, and long before him Saint Paul said: "Where sin increased, grace overflowed all the more."[3] We are like olives, the Talmud tells us: only when we are crushed do we yield what is of greatest value.

When the people of Israel returned from the Babylonian captivity, they brought back to their homeland the precious urge for spiritual renewal. For years I've been asking myself whether the nations who were crushed by totalitarian Communist regimes for decades brought something equally precious to the rest of Europe after they emerged from that night of oppression, or whether they might still be able to. Often I am tempted to reply that we disappointed those who expected something of the kind from us. Like the weary prophet Elijah we must admit that "we are no better than our fathers."

But after Easter this year I felt—and I'm sure I was not alone—that I could glimpse a light, which maybe was not sufficiently apparent to all when it was among us in the frail lantern of the body. Was not John Paul II, the pope from Poland, that light and signal of hope? A gift sent by God to Europe from the dark night of history and from the depths of suffering of crucified nations?

In saying this it is by no means my intention to fuel in a tawdry fashion the sometimes rather superficial "cult of personality" associated with that great pope. What I have in mind are two specific actions of enormous symbolic importance and consequence, two actions from which we here this evening might gratefully draw inspiration. In the first place I refer to that bold and humble act of confession and penitence for the Church's past faults, the pope's "Mea Culpa" at the beginning of Lent in the year of the millennium. And second, I am thinking of the great prayer gathering of representatives of world religions at Assisi.

I am deeply convinced that the twentieth century can leave in the memory of humanity two images of hope that may be a sign that it was not simply a century of historical darkness and suffering, but also a moment of change and hope. One is the photograph of the planet earth taken during the first human landing on the moon; the other is the photograph of the pope, holding hands with the Dalai Lama in the company of representatives of Judaism, Islam, and other world religions in front of the Basilica of St. Francis of Assisi.

Those two images have much in common. Not only does the photograph from the moon bear testimony to an enormous achievement of human courage and intelligence; it also shows how small our world is—just a little boat sailing through the endless darkness of the universe, "far away from all suns." And the image from Assisi is evidence of the hope that maybe we are beginning to realize that we have to learn to live together aboard this single frail vessel.

And so when we come to prayer together once again, here, near the grave of Saint Adalbert, bishop of my native city of Prague and patron of European unity, let us recall the prayer of Saint Francis by whose tomb the first of such gatherings took place: "Lord, make me an instrument of your peace!"

Let our minds and hearts embrace our entire history and let us pray for the healing of its painful wounds. Let us think of the victims of violence and hatred, in both our distant and our recent past, particularly those who were killed unjustly in the name of our God and in the presence of the holy symbols of our religions. "Victors write history," but God hears the lament of the victims and the vanquished. So we too should allow our hearts to listen to their call and be willing to remember not only the martyrs and victims within our own tradition, but also those in others' traditions.

The legacy of the faith of our father Abraham—belief in one God—unites us in one great family, and today we are aware of our mutual closeness. But God truly fulfilled his promise to Abraham that the number of his spiritual offspring would exceed the bounds of our imagination: they are as many as "the stars of the sky and the sands of the seashore"—and even in places we would not expect to find them.

As we look at the stars in the sky we think in our prayers tonight also of those who seem to be far, far beyond the bounds of our visible communities. Yet to God, who can "raise up children to Abraham from these stones," they are close.

Let us pray also for those who are unable to pray. They include some who have lost the strength to believe because of the dark night of history and the chasm of suffering; it is our duty to give them confirmation that the dawn is near. They include those who may not have recognized the face and name of our God—who, as the mystics of our three religions know, is a mysterious and hidden God—yet they join with us in rejecting false gods and oversimplified concepts of God.

"*Christians, Jews, Muslims, and atheists have this at least in common, that none of them believe in gods,*" a Christian theologian wrote recently. The God we believe in is not one of the gods of this world.

Yes, our shared service to this world lies also in our determined refusal to serve or adore the false gods of this world: "*Allahu akbar*"—God is the greatest—words heard several times a day in so many parts of the world from the lips of thousands of millions of our Muslim brothers and sisters. And their creed begins with the words: "There is no god but God."

There is no god (divinity) but God! This is something we ought to say all together and out loud to every corner of the globe: God is not in the storm or the whirlwind! God is not in the earthquakes of racial, ethnic, political, or religious hatred and intolerance! God is only in the "still, small voice"[4]—among "the peacemakers, for they will be called children of God."[5]

God is not in the destructive waves of the tsunami and other natural disasters but in the waves of solidarity with those who suffer.

There is no *holy war*—only peace is sacred. If everyone only followed the principle of "*an eye for an eye*" the whole world would soon be blind. We must break once and for all the dangerous spiral of vengeance and retribution. If our world is to be healed we can no longer rely on the logic of "as you have done to me so I'll do to you." We must learn the logic of "as God has done to me, so I'll do to you"—the path of forgiveness and reconciliation.

The strength to behave like that can come only from contemplation and prayer. May this evening's prayers reach all those places in the world where there is distress, where night still reigns; may they be a sign of hope that wherever people recognize brothers and sisters in one another—yes, also here among us—the dawn is breaking.

. 15 .

What Made Sarah Smile

A few years ago, a very close friend of mine confided in me that he no longer believed in life after death. I remember his precise words and the circumstances in which they were spoken.

We were climbing toward a massif in the high mountains. As I gazed at the amphitheater of mountains that suddenly emerged from the mist, I commented that that was more or less how I imagined the setting of the Last Judgment: each of us will stand atop a mountain peak, the highest point we have reached on our journey, with the valley of our entire life lying open below us, and we will answer the Lord's questions into the clouds. "I don't believe in it anymore" came the quiet—very quiet—response. "I haven't the strength to believe that there will be any afterward for me."

I sensed that this man, who had a deep and sincere belief in God, had just exposed to me one of his painful secrets. I refrained from unleashing a torrent of counterarguments. I felt that it was not his intention to table a debating issue, but that he was expecting me to share with him in silence the burden of what he had quietly told me. We remained silent as one does in the mountains and continued our climb.

In the period immediately following that mountain ascent I had a recurring dream. I dreamed that I had gone blind, and each time that I awoke in fright—before I was fully awake—I would stare into the total darkness and for a moment I would have the feeling that it had not been a dream but reality. The third time was the worst: at that moment of sudden awakening—I am sure everyone is familiar with that strange sense of vertigo on the threshold between dream and reality—for a split second I had the feeling that I was dying and falling, drawn down through a vortex of total darkness, into a bottomless void, into the maw of absolute emptiness, a definitive end that knows no afterward.

I immediately recalled that conversation in the mountains and I realized that it had affected me more than I was prepared to admit, probably because it had touched in me something that I had long suppressed. I have never felt real dread of death as nothingness and a radical end. Never before had I had any real problem with belief in life after death. I had accepted that article of the Creed along with the rest when, on the brink of adulthood, I became a believing Christian. I knew that it was pointless imagining anything by that mystery, and so it never became for me a particular matter for reflection or doubt. I am sure it was because I came to faith at an age when one's concerns are of a totally different order and one fondly believes that there is endless time to worry about eternity and "last things."

The friend who confided in me his disbelief in a personal prospect of eternity has returned to my memory once again. He is no naïve materialist but an intelligent and educated practicing Catholic. Often when people say "I don't believe" concerning matters of religion, they often mean by it that they "can't conceive of such a thing"; in his case it was a difficulty of a more serious and profound kind.

I respected the fact that he had not opted for any of the cheap wares available on the religious market these days—such as "belief in reincarnation," in order to tackle his problem with Christian eternity. Belief in reincarnation is something utterly alien to me, and I have several reasons to justify my radical rejection of it, particularly as regards the doctrine of reincarnation served up by Western esotericism. I don't reject those theories because my faith and imagination have been hemmed in by the dogmatic walls of some narrow-minded ideology, either a "scientific worldview" or some equally dubious Christian fundamentalism. I definitely have no intention of jumping to snap judgments about ancient traditions of Indian spirituality; besides, I am absolutely convinced that—at least in their more profound forms—these tenets have precious little in common with the popular notions that many people in the West have about the posthumous tourism of souls. After several conversations with Hindu and Buddhist scholars and gurus, I believe that for many of them the myth of reincarnation is more a poetic metaphor for the mystery of solidarity transcending the bounds of death—a mystery that we Christians render (also with the help of metaphor) by the doctrine of "purgatory" or "the communion of saints."

Yes, I freely admit that the mysterious solidarity that we confess in the Creed as the "communion of saints" goes much further and assumes more profound, subtler, and more intense forms than we are able to imagine. I do not rule out that the Platonic doctrine about the soul, which also influenced many early Christian authors, or the oriental myths about the cycle of destinies express a similar intuition and that those intuitions converge somewhere in the depths of that mystery. I am able to empathize with the sweet vertigo offered by oriental mysticism, wherein one contemplates being freed from the bonds of individuality and dissolving in the bosom of the deity. I am not willing, however, to surrender the greatest treasure of our Western culture—the concept of the personality—the incommutable value of the individual and the human person—as the supreme and most precious principle (such that we refer to God as a "person").

I believe that this "body" (that is, my incommutable being in time and space), my inimitable life story, and my unique personal individuality represent a task I was given by God and for which I will have to answer directly to God without any excuses about what went before and without endless scope for "having another go," or making reparations in future lives.

The main thing that irritates me about the "belief in reincarnation" that is now so widespread in the West is not its "content." After all, any theory or "notion" about things that happen after death—whether it be the materialists' belief in "the eternity of matter"; the popular Christian vision of heaven, purgatory, and hell; or these dreams of the Orient—relies on the language of metaphor and is burdened with all too human projections and fantasies. Even if we believe that something has been said or revealed to us "from the beyond," we know that even that message can speak to us only in images and metaphors. What irritates me most of all is the arrogance and naïveté with which the most ardent champions of "reincarnation" in the West speak about their belief. In the flashing eyes and affected voices of ladies with an interest in spirituality it is not hard to detect the shallowness of their noncommittal interest, which is more of a flirtation with titillatingly occult subject matter than a pursuit of anything resembling a conscientious spiritual journey.

I can't stand to hear someone talking about "reincarnation"—or, for that matter, about heaven, purgatory, and hell—with the proprietary manner of gnostic initiates: "I have it; it's now clear to me." It seems just as vapid and inane to me as when, with similar naïveté and arrogance, materialists invoke "science" in support of their "certainty" that death is the final end.

The fact is that we do not know. And the only thing I can add to that state of unknowing is my hope: I trust that even beyond that final frontier of my faculties, God will not let me fall into nothingness. The certainty of belief in "eternal life"— and the certainty of faith in general—differs fundamentally not only from the certainties that I can empirically "ascertain" but also from the esoteric "gnosis" of the gnostics, and the "convictions" of the devotees of ideological systems or "worldview" theories. The difference lies in the element that is constitutive for faith—the element of trust and hope.

The Gospel message about the Resurrection and the Church's corresponding belief in "the resurrection of the dead and the life everlasting" does not provide a "theory about life after death," as some kind of competitive variation on oriental mythologies, so that those like the aforementioned spiritualist ladies might choose the one they find most attractive. I do not seek within the Gospel a road map of the soul's posthumous fate, along the lines of the oriental "books of the dead"; I draw from it the power of the Spirit, which vitalizes the indestructible hope of our questioning—questioning that must always keep an open mind vis-à-vis the mystery, and which will probably be seized again and again by anxieties, sorrows, doubts, and uncertainties while we are still on our journey and have not yet reached our goal. Faith, unlike the "higher, secret knowledge" of the heirs of the gnostic insiders, is humble coexistence with Mystery; it feeds not only on the Word of God, but also on His Silence.

It is good that the editors of the Bible, guided by the wisdom of the Holy Spirit, censored nothing of that incredible range of different interpretations of man's posthumous fate that we find in the individual books of Scripture. There is a danger of shallow

one-sidedness in our popular "evolutionist" notion that the Old
Testament perspectives were "surpassed" by the subsequent pro-
nouncements of the Gospels: if by "surpassed" is meant "falsi-
fied" we would have to regard a large part of the Bible as not the
Word of God but instead an archive or mausoleum of refuted,
"invalidated" opinions. But that is not the case! As the most
profound Christian theologians and interpreters of Scripture
have known since the days of the Church fathers, between the
Hebrew Bible and the New Testament there is a "hermeneutic
circle": the Old Testament interprets the New Testament and
vice versa.

I am convinced that those who can handle the skepticism
that emanates from the Old Testament book of Ecclesiastes or
the darkness and hopelessness of Sheol spoken of in some of the
Psalms—and maybe such people alone—are capable of receiv-
ing as a liberating gospel (a joyful message of salvation and not
simply as a doctrine or theory) Jesus's profound words: "I am
the resurrection and the life; whoever believes in me, even if
he dies, will live" as well as the vision of the Resurrection in
the book of Revelation and Paul's letters. Those who make light
work of the crucified Christ's words from the abyss: "My God,
my God, why have you forsaken me"[1] will have difficulty appreciating the joy of the Easter morning.

The mystery of the Resurrection is not some external adden-
dum to the darkness of "death and hell." This idea was expressed
with great profundity by Joseph Ratzinger, the present Pope
Benedict XVI, in his book on eschatology, which I have found
very inspiring:

Christ Himself, the truly Just One, is in his very innocence,
He who undergoes suffering and abandonment even unto
death. The Just One descended into Sheol, to that im-
pure land where no praise of God is ever sounded. In the

descent of Jesus, God Himself descends into Sheol. At that moment, death ceases to be the God-forsaken land of darkness, a realm of unpitying distance from God. In Christ, God himself entered that realm of death, transforming the space of noncommunication into the place of his own presence.[2]

If we wish to meet with the Conqueror of death, we, too, cannot avoid that place (nor the likelihood that it will occasionally cast its shadow across our thinking). However, we can rely on the hope that He came through that darkness and by overcoming it, conquered it—and that is the only reason that death and its darkness does not have to be the gates of hell with the inscription *Lasciate ogni speranza*[3] but instead is the place where I will meet Him. That is the only reason that, at the end, I can overcome my fear of walking "through the valley of the shadow of death."[4]

The man I was walking with up that mountain path had not abandoned his belief in an afterlife recklessly. He had not exchanged a difficult article of faith for some shoddy belief or superstition, or for the materialist belief in the "eternity of matter" (that odd inversion of pantheistic mysticism), nor for the aforementioned pseudo-oriental reliance on an endless cycle of reattempts at life. I sensed that the source of his skepticism was to be sought elsewhere.

That man had experienced such pain and disappointment in his life that his capacity to trust had simply been extinguished. The repeated frustrations had convinced him that if any hope emerged that pointed beyond the last horizon of human life, he would simply fall prey to illusion once more. It seemed to him difficult or even impossible to rely on anything that promised some personal boon for him, and Pascal's wager on the possibility of immortality seemed to him simply a consoling trick. I know that he went through moments when it was almost a heroic act of loyalty to God and obedience to his faith that he stayed alive and "did not give God back his entrance ticket." I respected him greatly for that.

As I empathized with his situation and reflected on it I suddenly started to realize that my own belief in "last things" was full of darkness. A couple of times in my life I have had a "near brush with death," but at none of those extreme moments did death have the appearance of "not being." Up until the night I dreamed of death as nothingness I could foolishly imagine that such matters were purely of marginal interest, because they didn't particularly concern me (yet). Now I had to abandon those illusions. I realized that "last things" were not only "topical" in respect to the course of my life, but they were, moreover, far from marginal as regards my Christian faith.

In a sense, belief in "last things" is a kind of touchstone for the authenticity of our belief in God in general. If we restrict ourselves to the playing field of this life then maybe all we need of Christianity is what remained of it after the post-Enlightenment selling off of transcendence—a smidgen of moral principles and humanitarian kindness, a slightly updated version of existentialism, and a poetic sense of the mysterious. But when the curtain is about to fall on the stage of our earthly life, all of a sudden we are dreadfully alone in the auditorium—the god of such a humanitarian religion has disappeared through the trapdoor because he was too feeble to confront death.

"This world" either carefully avoids the issue of death or flirts with it noncommittally. It wants to "neutralize" it by means of the never-ending clichés of TV horror films, newsreel disasters, or the ornaments worn by rock musicians, and trivialize it by incorporating it into the entertainment industry. But when eventually the theme of death does appear on the scene in all its nakedness—and death is something that cannot be averted—it inevitably raises the question: Where is your God? Is there something in your life that allows you to relativize death?

A part of human suffering, a part of the cross of finite human existence, is the fact that one can be beset by severe doubts when confronted with the promises of eternal life. As I have already said, what I heard from my friend in the mountains that day was not the intellectual whim of someone consigning God's promises to the realm of fairy tales out of supercilious narrow-mindedness, or who, as the apostle Paul says, has "itching ears" and flits from one opinion to another and from one faith to another according to what religious wares are currently trendy.[5] If people's potential for trust and hope has been exhausted because of the pain they have suffered, it is up to us, their neighbors, not to assail their doubts with apologetic arguments, but instead to give them close support and encouragement to regain the courage to trust, to take that step of faith that says "and yet," "once more."

One of the great difficulties of believing in eternal life is that the prospect radically transcends the experience of any of us and is therefore *unimaginable.*

It is not easy to cope with the unimaginable, and regarding eschatological hope, Scripture states clearly that it concerns "what eye has not seen, and ear has not heard, and what has not entered the human heart."[6] And over the centuries the Church too has tried to give people an idea of the *unthinkable*; intellectuals used to receive refined theological theorizing while the "ordinary people" were served up the "paupers' Bible": pictures on church walls and in stained-glass windows that graphically illustrated the heaven, hell, and purgatory they heard about in the sermons. When he was describing souls being fried in hell and limbs being torn, Father Koniáš, one of my predecessors in the pulpit at the Church of the Most Holy Savior, would jangle chains, writhe, slobber, and swoon in ecstasy; the people loved it, probably experiencing the same blood-chilling and stomach-churning thrill as modern viewers watching a horror film. I remember from my youth how a certain notorious Redemptorist preacher, true to the tradition of his order, would not lose an opportunity to preach about the "last things"; at the feast of Corpus Christi he once described hell so luridly that some of the girls in front of the altar peed themselves in fright.

Although some Christian apologists and theological restorationists refuse to admit it, philosophical criticism, from Kant and Nietzsche through Wittgenstein, shattered the old, well-kempt academic metaphysical and theological systems. The tragedies of twentieth-century history (and of the first steps into the new century) have totally compromised and called into question human perceptions of the afterlife. After the experience of the Gulag, Auschwitz, Dresden, Hiroshima, Katyn, Srebrenica, the American prison at Abu Graib in Iraq, or the school at Beslan in the Caucasus, the old images of torment in hell seem pathetic, comical, and lacking in invention. Likewise, the traditional notions of heavenly delights seem dull compared to the wealth and scope of interesting possibilities in the modern-day world. In a lecture I gave in April 2004 at Mannheim,[7] in which I dealt with these issues in greater detail, I tried to outline the notion of a *negative eschatology,* which, analogous to "negative theology," would say only "what the last things *were not.*" Such a critique of all values that purport to be "the ultimate and supreme"—from political and social utopias to complete satisfaction and identification with the existing status quo in the life of society or the Church, or ideological (including theological) systems that claim to be a total expression of the entire truth—is certainly a fundamental prophetic component of faith: the demolition of models.

But can this negative eschatology help overcome the sorrow of being unable to believe "that there will be any afterward for me"? Can it calm me after I wake out of a dream that reveals naked anxiety about the abyss of nonbeing?

I have always found it odd and even comical when the Christian vision of eternal life is described as "a crutch" or "cheap solace." After all, according to Christian belief the first thing awaiting us beyond the gates of death is God's judgment. On the contrary, isn't "cheap solace" precisely the notion that death is the end of everything and we don't have to answer to anyone for our lives?

However, if we take seriously what the Gospels tell us about Christ, his judgment should certainly not resemble a "bugaboo for the misbehaved." Christ is the Truth, and to stand in the light of that truth (in the language of the Gospel, "truth," *aletheia,* means "the state of not being hidden") must truly be—or at least I've always sensed this—the pinnacle of our journey: one day we'll discover at last the entire and real truth about ourselves, about our lives and about everything that appertained to them; we'll hear at last the "solution" that eluded us in the thicket of unanswered questions, errors, and complex mysteries.

The eschatological character of our faith implies that we should leave matters open and *abstain from judgment.* I cannot be the judge of myself or my brother. I cannot, as long as I live on this earth, fully assess either the entire truth of my various actions and words and their consequences, or the import of my various complicated life situations, because they have always contained something that I do not know and cannot understand. I needn't even waste time and energy judging and passing judgment on the world around me: after all "the ruler of this world has been condemned."[8] The hope that not we but Truth itself will have the last word has always struck me as very liberating.

Maybe when "the question of last things" is raised, we should stay silent and abstain from skeptical opinions, cheap solace, and clever-clever "ready-made theories." It behooves us not to "know" but to wait. The underlying mode of our faith, love, and hope is *patience.*

Only when we truly fall silent will we be able to hear once more the voice that says to us: Fear not. I have conquered the world. I am the resurrection and the life. I am with you always, until the end of the age.

Fine words, but empty promises? From behind the tent awning—and from deep within ourselves—comes Sarah's skeptical laugh.[9] How could that be possible, seeing that we are not only adult already, but also too old for great expectations?

"Why did Sarah laugh?" Doesn't she realize that there is *"nothing too marvelous"* for the Lord to accomplish? And Sarah lies, because she is afraid. Her laughter was also an expression of her fear of trusting. "Yes, you did laugh," the Lord insisted.

You did laugh, the Lord tells us. But maybe He'll treat us the way He did our mother Sarah. Maybe our nervous laughter of skepticism and mistrust will be transformed into the happy laughter of those who have lived to see the fulfillment of His promises.

Second-Wind Christianity

As I read the still raw manuscript of this book after an interval of several days, I realize that in places there are references to the circumstances and place in which it was written—this hermitage, which I must leave once more. Wouldn't it be better to leave them out and let the text speak for itself without any distracting references to the person of its author and the surroundings in which it came into existence? No, my conviction is that by acknowledging the context in which these reflections evolved, I also give the reader a certain key to understanding them.

I write here not solely because I have more time, peace, and silence than in the bustle of Prague during the academic year, or because the weeks here in the hermitage also offer me immediate contact with nature, the rhythm of the liturgy, meditation, and work, as well as the facilities of the nearby monastery of a contemplative order. There is something more: I sense that something happens to me here. After a certain period of total isolation, silence, and the fixed order of prayer, I start to perceive, see, and think *differently* than I am able to in the course of my everyday duties. Self-mockery is something I practice all the time, and I have often cast an ironic gaze on this "playing the hermit" that I do every summer, but I've suddenly realized that this "game" is much more serious than the other games that destiny plays with me.

This year, now that I feel it more strongly than ever before, I am summoning up the courage to say it: over these recent years I have been undergoing a process of inner transformation; perhaps it could be described as "getting a second wind" in my life of faith. The issues dealt with in this book are not simply abstract or academic as far as I am concerned. I am trying to express my own personal spiritual experience, because I feel clearly—and I know so from my work as a confessor—that getting a second wind is not peculiar to me by any means.

Solitude and concentration are essential preconditions if one is to see things with a *fresh gaze*. In several places in this book I voice my reservations about the "new religious movements"— possibly with a touch of unfair irony. Among those reservations is the fear that amid the enthusiasm and warmth of a religious community people are unwilling to acknowledge the depth of the crisis in which the present form of "religion" finds itself. And if people fail to acknowledge and experience the depth of a crisis, they can also lose the opportunity to change and make a fresh start. The "new spring of Christianity" and the "new evangelization," the bromides that are frequently heard from such groups, involve—I fear—the risk that people will rely too optimistically on the thought that things are not too bad yet with the Church, that there are still youthful members, and so forth. But is that the most important thing? The question isn't how many of us there are, but whether or not we have lost our way.

Sören Kierkegaard, whom I regard as the first real prophet of the new path of faith—of faith as the courage to *live in paradox*—used to stress that in faith, people stand before God as *individuals*.[1] In his own loneliness, Kierkegaard experienced the paradox of which Jesus spoke: God is like the shepherd who left behind ninety-nine sheep and went off in search of "the one that was lost." Maybe today also God will tend to go after the "lost sheep," talk to their hearts, and carry them on His shoulders, accomplishing something out of their experience of "being lost and found again" that he could not achieve with the ninety-nine percent that never wandered, that is, those people who believe themselves to be in good health and therefore have no real need of Him—the doctor.

Yes, "the Church is a community," "Christianity is not private enterprise," and so on. We are all familiar with this rhetoric of the Church, and in a sense it is true, of course. However, I am increasingly convinced that the future face of the Church—a church that will fulfill the promise that "the gates of the netherworld will not prevail against it"[2]—will be more of a "community of the shaken"[3] than the sharing en masse of an unproblematized tradition that is accepted as a matter of course.

This is an era of tremors and upheavals, and there are worse to come. One of the great paradoxes that we will experience, and that we are already experiencing, is that the very part of the Church that all too glibly regards itself as a "stronghold," will, I fear, share the fate of the house that was built on sand.

Christian faith is a *renewed* act of belief in meaning, after we have experienced the total debacle of the latter. It is no mere mechanical return to what there was before, but requires the courage to trust at the point where we find ourselves beyond the bounds of what we can grasp and comprehend.

We usually define the "Christianness" of faith in terms of its "content" and "subject matter," of what is "narrative" in our faith, what is related to the story in which the message (*kerygma*) of Christianity is conveyed. But let us try for a moment to put all that "into brackets" and come down to the most fundamental, intrinsic structure of faith, to that *crystal lattice* inside the crystal, and by "crystal" here I mean both biblical texts and the entire treasury of symbols, dogma, and rituals that we encounter in the tradition and practice of the Church.[4]

The *paschal* character of Christian faith, which I spoke about in the first chapter of this book, resides in the experience of two "shocks." The first of these shocks is "the cross"—the *total loss of previous certainties,* "leaning out into the night of nonbeing";[5] such a debacle, however, can give rise to the "solidarity of the shaken."[6] The second tremor is confronting and overcoming the despair and resignation that one is tempted to fall prey to at moments of debacle, thereby finding *an assurance of a different order,* which slowly pierces—as a ray of *hope*—the darkness into which the shaken are plunged.

This is precisely the structure we find in the Easter story: it starts with the disciples' trust in Jesus (the story from their *calling* through to the *Last Supper*); then comes the drama of the Passion, which ends with both their defection ("Then all the disciples left him and fled"[7]) and their confrontation with Jesus's *debacle* (through to the final cry of "My God, why have you forsaken me?"[8]); and then the plunge into grief, despair, and fear ("the doors were locked, where the disciples were, for fear of the Jews"[9]). But then comes the second shock, the second shift: the road to Emmaus. An *unknown* fellow traveler listens to what they have experienced, their grief and their bitter questions. He lets them tell him everything before proceeding to relate to them *once more* the entire Bible narrative. He places in context their grievous experience; only *then* do they understand, and they gaze into the mystery ("their eyes were opened"[10]).

This "second moment of understanding" occurs at the "breaking of the bread,"[11] this repeated celebration of the Eucharist; thus the Eucharist stands at the beginning and the end of the Easter story—and during it Christ disappears from their sight, because they no longer need him in his former guise. They have the Eucharist as anamnesis—not simply as a "memento" in the sense of a souvenir or reminder of the past, but as a key to "understanding" that opens up the present moment both to the past (recalling Christ's sacrifice on the cross, as well as his "interpreting of the Law and the prophets"[12]) and also to an "absolute future" (being a "foretaste" of the banquet in the Kingdom of God).

It strikes me that we can discover this same schema over and over again as we examine our own lives. Max Weber regarded religion as a way of rationalizing the world. Savages who found themselves totally lost in the jungle with its thousands of dangers started to see a face or soul within natural phenomena;[13] in the course of evolution this vision was cultivated and the face of the deity became clearer and clearer and more reasonable (with a shift from natural religions to monotheism), until eventually reason (during the period of secularization and enlightenment) no longer needed any "sacred vehicle," and reason in nature and society was perceived simply as human rationality. But then, in a world that is *hominized but not humanized*—mechanized, bureaucratized, and alien, people again start to feel like savages lost in the jungle. This brief paraphrase of Weber's narrative could be developed and augmented, of course. At the summit of rational civilization not only do people feel anxiety in the face of its cold and complex inhumanity, but this inhumanity expresses itself as irrationality, which is a vital threat to humankind—there is no shortage of examples in our world.

Patočka used to speak about how, faced by the consequences of the misuse of technology for military ends, "*the shaken*" started to be roused, precisely among the foremost creators of technological civilization (and he cites as examples Oppen-heimer and Sakharov). They started to give precedence to the voice of *conscience* in place of relying on the automatic "prog-ress" of scientific rationality. Conscience, that "sense of mean-ing," also transforms human behavior from mere *reaction* (in which the "external"—"this world" in theological terms—is determinant) to *action* proceeding from within—from the con-science. *Kairos*, the opportune moment that is ripe for such a shift, is precisely the time in which humankind, as a result of the experience of World War I (that never actually ended, as Patočka maintained), is tilted out into the "night of nonbeing" and ceases to rely on the hitherto unquestioned truth of the "world of day"—a world governed by the logic and rationality of power.

Yes, in people's private lives also, a truly Christian "paschal faith" (unlike naïve, superficial religious observance with a ve-neer of Christian symbols and rhetoric) only generally comes into play as re-found faith—*second-wind faith.*

First the "original faith" is shaken or lost. This faith can be the "inherited Christianity of the fathers," a product of child-hood upbringing, or the initial fervor of the convert, or it can equally be simply the "original conviction" of a person who has no connection with Christianity or religion. This crisis and sev-erance of continuity can have various causes. It can be some traumatic disillusionment with those who imparted to us our original faith, or it can be a private drama, in which our original trust and certainties are eclipsed, or just simply a change of cir-cumstances and "mental climate."

Sometimes people lose their "youthful faith" as part of typical midlife depression, under the influence of the "noonday demon," known in the Bible as "the plague that ravages at noon"[14] (and by the monks and hermits of yore as the sin of *acedia*[15]); C. G.

Jung devoted a great deal of attention to this very phenomenon in his study of the individuation process in the course of his psychotherapeutic practice.[16] When I observe the weary Western European Christianity of our day I wonder whether those who share Teilhard de Chardin's optimistic conviction that "Christianity is still in its infancy" and those who, on the contrary, think it is obsolete and time-expired, are both mistaken. Maybe our Christianity is actually going through its midlife crisis, its "*acedia* phase," a time of lethargy and drowsiness.

But that would mean it is high time it woke up—albeit not in the manner proposed by the "trumpeters of Christianity"—and found its "second wind" and a readiness to *put out into the deep.*[17]

Maybe we won't encounter Christ where people tend to seek him first—in those aisles where he is offered like sale goods—but instead he will come to us like he did to the travelers on the road to Emmaus: as a *stranger*, an unknown fellow traveler, who first appears naïvely clueless about what we—and everyone else—is au fait with. And then we will have to let him *retell* the "great narrative" of the Bible to us.

We live in the "postmodern era," which has been described as a period marked by the end of the "great narratives."[18] However, it is also a period in which many narratives that are stored in our cultural memory are returning in new interpretations, placed into a new context.

Let us draw inspiration from the story of the road to Emmaus; only let us not content ourselves with mechanical references "backward" to Scripture and tradition, but listen afresh and more deeply to this narrative. Let us seek a new, deeper interpretation within the new context. On the road to Emmaus Jesus retells, that is, *reinterprets*, "*the great narrative of the Bible.*" He interprets it in the light of the travelers' present situation and state of mind, in answer to their questions, and in doing so, of course, he also reinterprets their present situation. He thereby radically transforms it—not by altering its outward components, but by changing their *understanding* and thus their attitude to the situation in which they find themselves. After all the human situation—unlike the *"Befindlichkeit"*[19] of things—is essentially shaped by the way people understand it, by their attitude to it.

Moreover, isn't one of the possible interpretations of the word *religio* based on the Latin verb *relegere,* to reread, to read with the potential of fresh understanding? Doesn't faith essentially consist of reinterpretation, of a *non-banal "reading" of life situations?*

I recall the crucial scene in Dostoyevsky's *Crime and Punishment,* in which Sonya is reading to Raskolnikov the Gospel passage about the resurrection of Lazarus. Not only do they both acquire a fresh understanding of this text from the point of view of their intolerable situation, but the text also helps them gain a fresh understanding of their life situations and allows them both, the murderer and the prostitute, to adopt a fresh attitude toward these situations. Here it is indeed a question of resurrection—*their* resurrection!

The apostle Paul never tires of repeating that if we have really come to believe in the Resurrection it means that we have *already been resurrected,* that we have risen again with Christ to new life. The gates to "new life" are a new and deeper understanding. The essence of conversion is a change of heart that enables one to see, understand, and live *anew.*

According to statistics, there is decreasing support for Christian churches in Czech society. Nevertheless an opposite trend can also be observed, a trend that I have personally witnessed as one who has had the privilege of accompanying many people on the path of conversion. Although it does not constitute a staggering percentage of the population, a considerable number of people in this country have been *returning* to religion, Christianity, and the Church in recent years. They have done so by finding somewhere a tiny opening into the world of faith that seems to them humanly and intellectually honest, and at least a bit "intelligible."

Intelligibility here is not a matter of primitiveness or simplification, but of someone speaking about faith in such a way that it *resonates* with their own experience. As a rule they do not encounter anything that is particularly surprising or "new" when the faith is preached in this way, but they feel that someone has managed to express precisely what they somehow already sensed long ago. The only thing that is new and surprising is to find it expressed from within the ranks of a church that is generally "written off" as obsolete.

Whether they are re-converts returning to the faith in which they were brought up or they are to which they once converted, and whose original belief died for some reason, or they are converts who have practically no experience of Christianity but are *returning* to it as to something in which they sense the beginnings and roots of their country's spiritual culture, I always try to demonstrate to them that a true spiritual "return" is not some kind of regression or step backward, but ought to be instead a step into the depths.

The value and sense of the journey show themselves in sundry ways on their return. If people return home after a long time away they usually see their home "with fresh eyes." In addition, the things that enriched them during their travels only become true riches after their return. Only in the safety and calm of home can the many things that have happened to us come to maturity as *experience*.

Sometimes I talk about "immediate Christianity" and "second-wind Christianity"; perhaps these are not the best descriptions, but I cannot think of anything better at this moment. Maybe Paul Ricœur had something similar in mind when he differentiated in religious belief between "primary naïveté" (which is no longer accessible to us) and "second naïveté" (which we might call "second immediacy"), which is a faith that has passed through the fire of rationalist critique and which, in his view, is only possible as an *interpretation* of religion (religious narratives and symbols).

Primary religiosity is often characterized by spontaneous enchantment with the world of the sacred; sooner or later, however, the moment usually arrives when one finds oneself outside the walls of that paradise.

I observe my five-year-old goddaughter Niké tapping on the wall to summon up from somewhere her alternative storybook identity; but sometimes she is sad that "it doesn't work anymore," that she is no longer able to transform herself instantly into a princess or Max and Sally.[20] Let her enjoy her storybook world, our psychologist friends urge, because soon, sometime on the threshold of school age, she will discover to her sorrow that that dimension of reality is closed off to her. The little boy in the delightful film *Shadowlands* seeks in vain the way into Narnia through the wardrobe in the attic of C. S. Lewis's house in Oxford.

It sometimes strikes me that we in the West treat our faith in a similar way. By kneeling at our bedsides at night or crossing the church threshold on Sunday we are also "tapping"—and at the agreed signal our pious self emerges and we enter the "realm of the sacred." *But sometimes it just doesn't work anymore.* Maybe we're in the same predicament as little Niké: we're approaching the age when that realm of treasures will be closed to us and we will knock in vain.

Maybe one day a "sacred time" will return again, when the

treasures will be revealed once more, such as on Good Friday in the cautionary Czech folk ballad, whose moral is that those who seek treasure with selfish and avaricious ends risk leaving their *child* behind: "the child within."

In comparing the "realm of the sacred" (what is *absolutely different* from our everyday world) to the world of children's fantasy I don't intend in the least to make light of the experience of the sacred.

In a sense, the world that is open to the child is richer and has greater variety and depth than our own; it is a bit like the *idios kosmos* (private world) of the *sleeper,* to which, according to Heraclitus, we return every night from the "shared world" of the wakeful. I sometimes have the impression that children have a greater ability than we have to move in various dimensions of reality "in parallel," and to move with no great difficulty from one world to another and retain them both at the same time without conflict. This afternoon, little Niké *is* Max, with an earnestness that excludes any notion of "pretense," and she requires of us consistently that we should respect this truth. She makes it plain to us that if we accept these rules, then she is *simultaneously* part of our world and will communicate with us when it is absolutely necessary, "in our language." It is only we who think that children's entire Christmas myth would disintegrate if they caught their parents in the act of putting presents under the Christmas tree on behalf of Baby Jesus.[21] Only *we* fondly imagine that the truth must be *either* this *or* that.

The anthropologist Paul Veyne wrote something similar in his remarkable book *Did the Greeks Believe in Their Myths?*[22] It was no problem for people in the ancient world to relate to some object or creature as a sacred reality one moment and treat it in a secular and pragmatic manner the next. It is only secular people of modern times who believe that it is necessary to choose one or the other alternative, because they have lost the sense of the world's paradoxical nature and the multidimensional character of reality.

Children do not speculate on logic or the concept of truth, but their world is so rich that it is able to encompass paradoxes without problem, and *paradoxes are not yet perceived as such*—just as in dreams we have no problem with someone being a dog and an uncle simultaneously, or I can happily accept that someone is dead and seated at table with me. As I observe Niké-Max, I regret that her world will soon become simplified and that play will be separated from "reality" by the use of the disparaging word "pretend." I likewise regret on waking that I am unable to hold on to a dream that wanted and was able to tell me more than I am able to cram into these pigeonholes of my mind that I'm accustomed to working with—and that it is only a sign of my helplessness when I brush it aside and tell myself it was "only a dream."

When the thinkers of the Enlightenment proudly declared that they had established the age of reason as an age of adulthood, and consigned religion to the world of children's fairy tales, they were right in a way. It is just odd that they did so with such cocky adolescent pride and did not stop to wonder whether they might not lose something in the process. Indeed the romantic age that followed close on its heels found the Enlightenment's choice of the "daytime world" one-sided and the light of reason too cold. The romantics tried to find a way of entering the world of dream and night: the doorway was to be *feeling, sensibility, emotion*—hence the sentimental religion of the romantics, and not just the romantics of the last century but one. But wasn't the sentimental religion of the romantics simply a game, a "pretend religion" or "pretend faith," rather than a genuine restoration?

When she grows up a bit, Niké will also be unable to return to the multidimensional world in which *everything was possible* via the doors of childish imagination. Maybe she will look for other ways into it sometimes, when "this world" proves too constraining. This world is sometimes too constraining for all of us—if it weren't, a lot of things wouldn't exist, from art to drugs.

I have not the slightest intention of romantically exalting the child's world of imagination above the adult world of reason. I simply want to show that the child's imagination is *one* gateway into the *dimension of mystery,* the transcendence of reality. After all, the world is much bigger than it appears to us; reality conceals an infinitude of variations and possibilities that seem like impossibilities to our reason and to our customary stereotypical thinking.

The theme of the impossible plays a very important role in the work of Jacques Derrida, the leading exponent of postmodern philosophy, who drew inspiration from the tradition of mysticism and negative theology. Derrida maintained that the possible emerged from the realm of the impossible; the *possible,* in his view, is everything that is predictable or can be planned, and so forth, while the *impossible* is what radically transcends the possibilities *under our control,* which lie within the present horizons of our reason and imagination.

Children are unaware of the treasure that is available to them, while those who have just passed their examination in the art of "worldly wisdom" generally do not appreciate how little they know of it in reality. Nicodemus's comment that "Surely [a man] cannot reenter his mother's womb and be born again, can he?"[23] certainly applies. When Jesus tells him "you must be born again," and in another passage he tells his disciples that "anyone who will not receive the kingdom of God like a little child will never enter it," he is definitely not urging us to become infantile.[24]

It is impossible for us to simply return to our childhood faith; *that* entrance to the "realm of the impossible" is truly sealed off for us. Maybe the biblical image of a paradise from which we were banished and which is now guarded by angels with flaming torches *also* has something to do with this "human situation."[25] We cannot become children again, just as Niké one day won't be able to become Max anymore—we can only be *like* children. To understand and fulfill this *analogy* is to search for *a different* access to the "impossible."

We cannot simply go back to before the adulthood that the era of Enlightenment brought us, and we should be wary of passing one-sided judgments on it. Romantic excursions into the world of the sacred—from the days of European romanticism to those who nowadays try to react to the "disappearance of the sacred" from our culture and from their own lives by regressing to their childhood faith or to imitations of the premodern Church, piety, and theology—are illusions (as demonstrated on several occasions in this book). By and large these attempts are a source of enjoyment and sometimes even look very nice—and certainly they can be necessary and useful on occasions. But they are illusions. A living, real faith, just like real life, cannot stand on the thin ice of illusion, through which we gaze or tumble into the depths of our "primal religiosity," because this time we could really end up drowning in those sacred depths; it is also possible that if we wander off into a world of open treasures of the sacred we risk leaving behind the "adult" in us when we re-emerge. Rationality too is a rare gift that we ought not rid ourselves of lightly!

As we meditate on the paths of our own cognition we can perhaps discern a certain analogy with the paschal experience that is the basic paradigm of Christian faith. We have long believed that we are uncovering "objective laws," whether in nature or in history. For some this work was proof that the world was so rational that it required no "God hypothesis"; for others it was "the piety of thinking," captivation with uncovering the traces of God in the world.

Now, in this postmodern era, many have reached the conclusion that all "objectivity" was an illusion and that the "laws" of nature and history were our own construct that we projected onto reality for ease of navigation. Attempts to capture in our net of rationality the infinitely profound, complex, and polymorphous "spaces" that we now see are undoubtedly doomed to fail. Nietzsche would seem to have been the first—as he was in many other things—to realize the problematic fragility of the "spiders' webs of reason," and he truly, profoundly understood that every perception is limited by the perspective of the perceiver, and every opinion, indeed every contemplation and observation, is *of itself interpretation.* It is impossible for us to attain "the reality about ourselves" entirely separate from our own involvement and our cognitive activity; we cannot step *beyond* our interpretation; the only way for us to broaden our own perspective is through dialogue with others.

This failure of modernism, the loss of its naïveté, and the process of "enlightening the enlightenment" are some of the more valuable outcomes of this phase of the Western intellect's historical journey. What was long ago apparent to the "negative theology" that grew out of mystic experience must now evidently be taken seriously in all spheres of our knowledge: reality is disproportionately "bigger" than our notions, words, categories, and perceptions. The way forward leads solely through paradoxes.

If reality were as flat as it appeared to the materialism and positivism of the modern era, and if the world were the "surface of the world" that we, inspired by Saint John's Gospel, call "this world," then the atheists and agnostics would be absolutely right: in such a world there is no God; we could not encounter Him there. To speak about God assumes *perceiving reality differently,* not being satisfied with the "surface" but also taking into account "the depths." However, we must be very cautious in our use of this spatial analogy. We must take great care not to tumble into either the naïveté of classical metaphysical realism, the "next-worldliness" of Platonism and Indian mythologies—or "subjectivism." There are not *two* "objectively existing" worlds—the changeable world of the surface on the one hand, and the real world of depth "beyond it" on the other.

There is one reality that is infinitely diversiform—and what we testify to are the fruits of various points of view, different perspectives, different experiences. What we metaphorically describe as "the surface," or using the biblical expression, "this world" (*saeculum*), is not something that "objectively exists," but is the product of a specific view of the world; it is a specific interpretation of reality. From a certain standpoint, in the framework of a specific way of life and attitude to reality, the world appears as "*saeculum.*"

But doesn't something similar apply to what we call "depth," the Kingdom of God, the sacred, "the realm of the impossible"? Even in this case we are not referring to some "objective reality" to which we might have access—other than via faith, love, and hope.

God is "present" and "visible" in the world in the acts of faith, love, and hope of people who believe—not as an *entity* that can be apprehended in some other way. Those who stand "outside the faith" can maybe catch a glimpse of what we call God in the witness of believers (that is, acts of faith, hope, and, above all, love)—although they will most likely use another vocabulary than the traditional language of faith to interpret and describe what they maybe glimpsed.

But not even believers themselves can experience God other than in acts of faith, love, and hope. Among present theologians,

Joseph Ratzinger in particular always emphasized strongly that faith could not be understood in the same sense as a mathematical formula and cannot be "rationally demonstrated" apart from the *experiment of life,* consisting of the path of faith, love, and hope: "The truth of Jesus' word cannot be tested in terms of theory. It is like a technical proposition: it is shown to be correct only by testing it. The truth of what God says here involves the whole person, the experiment of life. It can only become clear for me if I truly give myself up to the will of God. . . . This will of the creator is not something foreign to me, something external, but is the basis of my own being."[26]

When I maintain that there is no other path to God than the way of faith, it is absolutely not my intention to reduce or degrade God to a "merely subjective" entity. The underlying feature of this human experience of faith—if it truly is faith—is precisely the realization that *God is something that infinitely transcends the entire capacity of all human acts,* and to seek to reduce God to something "entirely human" would mean replacing God with an idol.

After the collapse of naïve metaphysical realism, which was the basis for a certain sort of rigid theology of the modern era, and also the collapse of the positivist concept of science and scientific knowledge, we are in a situation of *conflicting interpretations.* Here I fully subscribe to "postmodern" thinking that rejects the modern era's division of reality into "subjective" and "objective," and instead takes seriously the plurality of perspectives on the world. Reality stands before us as an inexhaustible mystery, full of paradoxes, open to many different interpretations—and the interpretation we choose is a matter of personal choice, risk, and responsibility.

However, if we choose the interpretation of the world that I denote by the word *faith,* a great paradox awaits us: we realize that our faith is not merely *"our* affair" (*merely* our choice), but that it is already *an answer to a challenge that preceded it.* "It was not you who chose me, but I who chose you," Jesus says.[27]

The *Catechism of the Catholic Church* characterizes faith similarly as a dialogue: God Himself places "metaphysical disquiet" within the human heart, the need to seek *meaning*, and God responds to this questioning with His Revelation; and people then respond—by an act of trust and self-surrender: their faith—to that divine sharing, the Word, wherein God gives Himself.

The extinction of many concepts of God that emerged in the modern era, such as the Great Watchmaker of the Universe, which the deists of the Enlightenment managed to sneak in to replace the mystery of the Trinity (and which, alas, many Christians failed to notice), also has an impact on spirituality and the spiritual lives of believers. Many of today's Christians—if I may refer to my experience as a confessor—are experiencing "a crisis of prayer": they are no longer able to remain present in all sincerity when simulated dialogue with an Invisible Uncle is interspersed with pious poems. It is necessary for us Christians to learn *contemplation* once more: the art of inner silence, in which God will be able to speak to us *through our own lives* and His unique events. Then life itself will act as a corrective should we try to indulge in pious trickery. Putting one's own projections and plans into God's mouth is possible only in the case of a make-believe god "in the wings." Happily, the living God—*the deep-down mystery of reality,* cannot be treated this way.

Isn't the most important mission of the confessor, who accompanies others on their spiritual journeys, to teach them the art of being silent and attentive, to distinguish and identify God's ciphers in the events of their own lives and to *respond to His challenges through their own lives?*

.   .   .

Much of what burdened me in those "confessor's nights" has slowly become clearer here in this time of solitude and contemplation, in this "hermit's morning." Yes, it is still *very early* morning—the first light of dawn; it is still a long time to go before the full, bright light of day. Will I live to see it in this lifetime, in this world?

The religion that is now disappearing has tried to eliminate paradoxes from our experience of reality;[28] the faith we are maturing toward, a paschal faith, teaches us *to live with paradoxes*. Let us not fear the upheavals that the present epoch will bring, even upheavals in the field of religion. Much is disappearing and much more will disappear. However, something will remain on which to build—as I firmly believe—"a second-wind Christianity": faith, hope, and love, these three. For the era on whose threshold we stand, my guess is that hope will be what is needed most of all.

Notes

1: The Confessor's Night

1. Matthew 19:26.
2. 2 Corinthians 12:10.
3. Let us not forget that in the mother tongue of the Gospels *methodos* means "a way."
4. Out of the entire gamut of predictions of its demise that have accompanied Christianity through twenty centuries I would recall, for instance, the exchange of letters between Voltaire and Frederick of Prussia, who, in the mid-eighteenth century, were convinced that the Christian religion would disappear from the world within fifty years at most (cf. Ben Ray Redman, *The Portable Voltaire* [New York, 1949], p. 26).
5. I find a hint of this kind of "deep theology" in the writings of the Jewish theologian Abraham Heschel (1907–1972), who shows how, in the modern depersonalized world, even God has been reduced to "something for our use," which has led to the banalization of religion. It is therefore necessary to dive deep beneath those structures and rediscover a sense of mystery, wonder, and awe.
6. The full text of the absolution is as follows: "God the Father of mercies, through the death and resurrection of his Son, has reconciled the world to himself and sent the Holy Spirit among us for the forgiveness of sins; through the ministry of the Church may God give you pardon and

peace, and I absolve you from your sins in the name of the Father, and of the Son, and of the Holy Spirit."

7. Acts 17:22–34.

8. See, for instance, Romans 6:9: "Christ, raised from the dead, dies no more."

9. As theologians emphasize, the word of the Greek text of the New Testament that we translate as "resurrection" is taken from the experience of people waking from sleep and of "resuscitation," the return to this life after apparent death. It can therefore only serve as an analogy or metaphor for the mystery of Christ's victory over death, which Christian belief interprets as something radically different and more profound. (It would be a total misapprehension if our drawing attention to the limitations of this concept were taken as a diminution of the Easter mystery—the opposite is true.)

10. A note for theologian colleagues: *the Theology of Paradox* rejects any "nothing buts" and espouses the principle of "not only but also." So one cannot even say of the Resurrection that it is "nothing but" a reinterpretation of the cross; otherwise we'd find ourselves in the shallows of old liberal theology. The opposite one-sidedness, the view that the Resurrection is "nothing but" a historical event among other historical events, or a "miracle" among other miracles, leads to the abyss of fundamentalist banality. The Resurrection is an event of an *eschatological* character—that is indicated by the expression "the third day," which is not simply a chronological fact—bursting into time; it needed time to penetrate the hearts and minds of the disciples and bring light thereto, enabling them also to understand the meaning of Christ's suffering and cross.

11. See *Love's Strategy: The Political Theology of Johann Baptist Metz*, ed. John K. Downey (Harrisburg, PA: Trinity Press International, 1999).

12. Perhaps this is stated most explicitly in the letter of James (James 2:18–26) and Jesus's parable about the Last Judgment (Matthew 24:31–46).

13. Sigmund Freud–Oskar Pfister, Sigmund Freud, *Psychoanalysis and Faith: Dialogues with the Reverend Oskar Pfister* (New York: Basic Books, 1963), p. 122.

14. Perceptions of "the natural" and the "supernatural" will be dealt with in particular in chapter 9, "A Rabbit Playing the Violin."

15. More about this in chapter 3, "Kingdom of the Impossible Come."

16. John 14:12.

17. Romans 4:18.

2: Give Us a Little Faith

1. Luke 17:5–7.

2. What often comes to mind here is a philosophical essay by Ernst Jünger, *Der Waldgang* (excerpts translated into English under the title "The

Retreat into the Forest," in *Confluence: An International Forum* 3, no. 2 (1954): 127–42, in which the "forest walker" is the author's proto-type of the human individual, who, at a time of increasing "automatism," preserves his original attitude to freedom; at one time this book greatly inspired me with its words about the priest, who at a time of persecu-tion and spiritual deserts, has no option but this "forest existence" as a source of strength to assuage people's hunger for authentic living.

3. See Mark 11:22. In most translations this is rendered as "have faith in God," while the literal meaning, preserved in the Czech Kralice transla-tion (and the Wycliffe translation) is as here (translator's note).

4. See 1 Corinthians 1:19–30, and so forth.

3: KINGDOM OF THE IMPOSSIBLE COME

1. Luke 17:6.

2. Of course one cannot indiscriminately associate all movements that em-phasize the work of the Holy Spirit with these "raving charismatics." Moreover there are certain signs that even in the "Pentecostal move-ment," which emerged within American evangelical circles and has spread across to other denominations, the phase of "raving charismatics" is simply a passing phase, "an infantile disorder."

3. Richard Rorty, *Achieving Our Country: Leftist Thought in Twentieth-Century America* (Cambridge, MA: Harvard University Press, 1998), p. 22.

4. There are innumerable philosophical and theological interpretations of the notion of "this world" such as it is used in John's Gospel: it is the antithesis of the Kingdom of God, a world "which lies in evil." This is not some pseudo-platonic disparagement of "secularity" in the name of some sort of "world beyond," world of ideas, and so forth. We could maybe explain the expression "this world" by reference to Heidegger's description of "fallenness" (*Verfallenheit*), "inauthentic existence," an ir-responsible, "dispersed" life on the surface as one lives (*man lebt*) in the world. Paul the apostle uses the dichotomy "living according to the Spirit" and "living according to the flesh" to describe these two ways of living.

5. It is definitely not fortuitous that Luke's Gospel places Jesus's words about the need to forgive over and over again just before his statement about the mustard seed.

6. John 18:36.

7. Matthew 19:26.

8. See Genesis 18:14; Luke 1:37; and so forth.

9. Matthew 13:31–32.

10. See Romans 7:14–25.

11. To appease those who adhere to one of the theological definitions of the First Vatican Council, and the neo-scholasticism that was inspired by

that dogma, I would add that I too agree that the path of human reason, or, more exactly, rationality of a certain type, can lead to the assurance that there exists a sovereign power that we may term "God," the Creator, and so on; let us leave aside for now the discussion about the relationship of this "god of the metaphysicians" to God, who displays Himself *solely* in love and hope and because of those divine virtues is also immersed in the impenetrable light of inexhaustible mystery.

12. See Luke 5:1–11.
13. Matthew 19:25–26.

4: Intimation of the Presence

1. In French, the word *milieu* can mean middle or environment.
2. It was certainly not fortuitous that Teilhard chose this favorite expression of Nietzsche's from his book *Thus Spake Zarathustra*.
3. Jan Patočka, *Heretical Essays in the Philosophy of History*, ed. James Dodd, trans. Erazim Kohák (Chicago: Open Court, 1999).
4. This statement by Saint Cyprian (d. 285) was originally directed against the Rigorists, who denied the validity of the baptism of believers who had dropped away when the Church was persecuted. It is worth noting that the interpretation of this sentence in the sense of "those who are not members of the Catholic Church cannot be saved" was rejected by the Vatican's Holy Office of August 8, 1949, as heretical; indeed for espousing this heresy the American priest Father Leonard Feeney, SJ, was excommunicated by Pope Pius XII on February 5, 1953.
5. Hans Urs von Balthasar, *Elucidations* (San Francisco: Ignatius Press, 1998).
6. Ibid., emphasis added.
7. 2 Corinthians 12:10.
8. Cf. Nehemiah 8:10.

5: Discreet Faith

1. Nicholas Lash, *Holiness, Speech and Silence: Reflections on the Question of God* (Farnham, Surrey, UK): Ashgate Publishing Group, 2004), p. 84.
2. See Luke 9:28–36.

6: The Tribulations of a Believing Scientist

1. This reference to Sartre is not intended, of course, to compare certain official structures of our church with hell. Nevertheless, the Sheol of the Old Testament, the sad realm of shadows, where it is hard to praise the Lord, or the *limbo* that was invented by those who had

misunderstood the principles of "extra ecclesiam" as a place of punishment/non-punishment for unchristened babies has been evoked for me most vividly by various talks or conferences in such circles.

2. Werner Keller, *The Bible as History* (New York: Bantam Books, 1983).

3. Professor Lash's philosophy is dealt with more extensively in the chapter "A Rabbit Playing a Violin."

4. Probably the first person to develop this idea was Michael Buckley, SJ, in his book *At the Origins of Modern Atheism* (New Haven, CT: Yale University Press, 1990).

5. See more on this theme in chapter 5.

6. See James 2:18.

7. Lash, *Holiness, Speech, and Silence,* esp. pp. 78–85.

7: The Joy of Not Being God

1. "If you (fully) comprehend, it is not God" (Saint Augustine, Sermo 1.17);that is, God is incomprehensible.

2. Cf. Romans 5:12–21.

3. Regarding the "selfism" of contemporary civilization, see, for example: Gilles Lipovetsky, *L'ère du vide: Essais sur l'individualisme Contemporain* (Paris: Gallimard, 1999); and Paul C. Vitz, *Psychology as Religion: The Cult of Self-Worship* (Grand Rapids, MI: Eerdmans, 1994).

4. Cf. John 16:11.

8: There and Back Again

1. Jiří Langer, *Nine Gates,* trans. Stephen Jolly (Cambridge, U.K.: Lutterworth Press, 1987). On account of Langer's book I myself "disappeared" into the world of Chassidic legends for a few years at one point, rather in the way that my former student disappeared into his Buddhist monastery.

2. See Luke 15:11–32.

3. See the document *Nostra Aetate* of the Second Vatican Council.

4. 2 Corinthians 4:7.

5. Perhaps this is expressed most beautifully in Colossians 1:15–20.

6. 1 Timothy 3:15.

7. This expression as a "definition of the Church" appears in the documents of the Second Vatican Council (in the dogmatic constitution *Lumen Gentium*).

8. Cf. 1 Corinthians 13:12 and elsewhere.

9. Cf. John 20:28.

10. Cf. John 20:11–18.

9: A Rabbit Playing the Violin

1. Nicholas Lash, *Holiness, Speech and Silence.*
2. See also chapter 6: "The Tribulations of a Believing Scientist."
3. Lash, *Holiness, Speech and Silence*, pp. 44–45.
4. Ibid., p. 10.
5. Ibid., p. 14
6. Ibid., pp. 14–15.
7. Fergus Kerr, *After Aquinas: Versions of Thomism* (London: Wiley-Blackwell, 2002) p. 190.
8. Also known as Matthias (d. 1394), he was appointed canon and confessor at Prague Cathedral in 1381 (trans.).
9. Aka Adalbertus Ranconis (c. 1320–August 15, 1388), he was rector of the Sorbonne in 1355 (trans.).
10. I dealt with this possibility at length in my book *Vzýván i nevzýván: Evropské přednášky k filosofii a sociologii dějin křest'anství* [*Bidden and Unbidden: European Lectures on the Philosophy and Sociology of the History of Christianity*] (Prague: Nakladatelství Lidové noviny, 2004).
11. More on that in chapter 5, "Discreet Faith."
12. Most likely we shall see the fulfillment of Rahner's prediction that the Christianity of the new millennium will be either *mystical* or nonexistent.

10: God Knows Why

1. Cf. Proverbs 8:31.

11: Living in the Visual Field

1. Exodus 23:2.

12: I Cry Out: Violence!

1. Most of the cheap anti-Christian trash on the stage, in galleries, and on the book market, which, in the normal course of events, would rightly sink without trace overnight, is created precisely because the authors count on vehement protests on the part of certain Christian circles to ensure the books' market success and possibly their reputation as "bold works"—and they are never disappointed. If, however, the works go over the top and offend Jews and Muslims, too, the Western authorities immediately step in and the offending works are often confiscated and the author penalized or at least required to apologize for his intolerance and

insult to religion. On the other hand, if they insult only Christianity in a similar or even more blatant fashion, the same authorities will defend the authors in the name of artistic freedom and free speech. We live in an odd world.

13: THE SIGN OF JONAH

1. The name of the bureaucrats' artificial language in Václav Havel's play *The Memorandum* (San Francisco: Grove, 1990).
2. Matthew 12:39.
3. Jonah 4:1–11.

14: THE PRAYER OF THAT EVENING

1. This text was delivered at the opening of a memorable joint prayer gathering by leading representatives of Judaism, Christianity, and Islam during the international conference "The Europe of Dialogue," held in Gniezno, Poland, September 16–18, 2005. The title is taken from an article by Karel Čapek, which was an immediate reaction to the Munich Agreement of 1938.
2. From the poem "Patmos," in Friedrich Hölderlin, *Hyperion and Selected Poems*, ed. Eric L. Santner (New York: Continuum, 1990).
3. Romans 5:20.
4. 1 Kings 19:9–13.
5. Matthew 5:9.

15: WHAT MADE SARAH SMILE

1. Such as by making the banal (though admittedly factual) point that it is a quotation from Psalm 22 "which has an optimistic ending."
2. Joseph Ratzinger, *Eschatology: Death and Eternal Life* (Washington, DC: Catholic University of America Press, 2007).
3. "Abandon All Hope"—the sign above the gates to hell according to Dante's *Divine Comedy*.
4. Cf. Psalm 23:4.
5. 2 Timothy 4:3.
6. 1 Corinthians 2:9; and cf. Isaiah 64:3.
7. In Tomáš Halík, *Vzýván i nevzýván* [*Bidden and Unbidden*].
8. John 16:11.
9. Cf. Genesis 18:12–15.

16: SECOND-WIND CHRISTIANITY

1. Here faith is a journey that was first undertaken by the "father of the faith," Abraham, and was preached by the prophets; unlike—I would add—"religion," for which the vehicle is always society (tribe, nation), tradition, and authority.

2. Matthew 16:18.

3. This is the term used by the Czech philosopher Jan Patočka (1907–1977) in his last and crowning work, *Heretical Essays in the Philosophy of History.*

4. My inspiration here is the simile that C. G. Jung liked to use to clarify the relationship between the archetype (the crystal lattice within the crystal) and the symbol (the "body" of the crystal), which I think can usefully demonstrate the inseparability of the two: the crystal lattice cannot be encountered outside the crystal, that is, the archetype outside of the symbol. Likewise, this inner structure of faith cannot be encountered outside the setting in which faith "happens," whether by this we mean its narrative component (Scripture and tradition), the symbols of celebration (the liturgy), or how people experience or bear witness to it in their lives (*diakonoia* and *martyria*).

5. Another image borrowed from Jan Patočka's *Heretical Essays.*

6. See previous note.

7. Matthew 26:56.

8. Matthew 27:46.

9. John 20:19.

10. Luke 24:31.

11. Luke 24:35.

12. Cf. Luke 24:27.

13. Whether they *projected* it there or *found* it there is a matter we can leave to one side.

14. Psalm 91:6.

15. In the popular catalogue of sins, *acedia* (the seventh of the "capital sins") is inaccurately translated as "sloth"; whereas in fact it is a certain form of disgust, *taedium vitae,* world-weariness and resignation. Were we to psychologize or psychiatrize this spiritual quality—whereby we would somewhat trivialize the issue—we would probably diagnose it as "burnout syndrome."

16. Jung maintains that around the symbolic midlife point (generally after the thirty-fifth year of life), many people experience some kind of crisis—family, relationships, work, health—or they develop a vague aversion to everything they have achieved hitherto and to their previous motivations. The crisis has a purpose, however; it is to warn people not to spend the second half of their lives building the external facade of their selves (that is, concentrating on careers or property, because building a "visible base" of our existence—and not only in the narrowly material sense—is more an activity for the "morning of our lives"), and

to instead finally set out on the arduous and risky journey inward, the spiritual journey of ripening and seeking one's "higher Self" (*das Selbst*).

17. Cf. Luke 5:4.

18. Cf. Jean-François Lyotard, *La Condition Postmoderne*. Les Éditions de Minuit. Paris, 1985.

19. The expression used by Heidegger to denote how people sense themselves in situations.

20. For those not in the know: Max, Sally, and the dog, Jonathan, are characters in a Czech children's TV show.

21. In Czech tradition, Christmas presents come from the infant Jesus and appear beneath the Christmas tree at nightfall on December 24 (translator's note).

22. Paul Veyne, *Did the Greeks Believe in Their Myths?: An Essay on the Constitutive Imagination,* trans. Paula Wissing (Chicago: University of Chicago Press, 1988).

23. John 3:4.

24. Nor, for that matter, is he referring to "reincarnation" as some theological dabblers have interpreted it. The system of karma is entirely alien to the work of the Bible, and the esotericists' endlessly repeated invention that later councils expunged from the Bible and teachings of the early church the original articles of the faith relating to reincarnation are a nonsense that is as impossible to prove (or refute) as the Muslims' assertion that the Koran contains a "more original version" of Jesus's life than the Gospels. They probably stem from distorted accounts of the Church's condemnation of some of the neo-platonic elements in Origen's teaching.

25. Or to look at it from the opposite perspective: when one passes from childhood to adulthood, one "repeats," in a sense, this *primeval* experience of the history of salvation.

26. Pope Benedict XVI; *God and the World: A Conversation with Peter Seewald* (San Francisco: Ignatius, 2002).

27. John 15:16.

28. The sociologist Niklas Luhmann, in particular, spoke about religion as *Entparadoxierung* ("deparadoxification"). Cf. Niklas Luhmann, *Funktion der Religion: Suhrkamp taschenbuch wissenschaft* (Berlin: Suhrkamp, 1977).

About the Author

TOMÁŠ HALÍK worked as a psychotherapist during the Communist regime in Czechoslovakia and at the same time was secretly ordained as a Catholic priest and active in the underground church. Since the fall of the regime, he has served as General Secretary to the Czech Conference of Bishops and was an adviser to Václav Havel. He has lectured at many universities throughout the world and is currently a professor of philosophy and sociology at Charles University. His books, which are bestsellers in his own country, have been translated into many languages and have received several literary prizes. He has been awarded various prizes worldwide, including the prestigious Romano Guardini Prize for "outstanding merits in interpreting contemporary society" (2010) and the prize for the best European theological book (2009–2011) for his book *Patience with God*, which was also selected as "book of the month" in August 2010 by the National Catholic Book Club in the United States.

Printed in the United States
by Baker & Taylor Publisher Services